Success guides

CRAIG ROBERTSON

Intermediate 1
Hospitality

Edna Hepburn ✗ Jean McAllister

Contents

Food Hygiene for the Hospitality Industry

Using this book

The information in this book should help you make good progress through the Intermediate 1 Hospitality: Practical Cookery course and so help you achieve the best possible grades.

Food safety and hygiene play an important part in all your practical activities, so there is a separate chapter on this topic at the beginning of the book – but remember that this topic will also be covered in some way in each unit.

The other chapters in the book are arranged to cover the course content of the four units in the Intermediate 1 course.

At the start of each chapter is a section called **'What's this unit all about?'** These pages will give you information on:

- the outcomes (what you have to do) for each unit
- the assessments for each unit
- what you have to know or do to pass each assessment.

At the end of each chapter, you will find **assessment practice**. These pages will give you an opportunity to practise the types of activity you will find in your National Assessment Bank items (NABs), issued by the Scottish Qualifications Authority (SQA). You have to pass the National Assessment Bank items, so it is a good idea to have some practice first.

Answers for the assessment practice are found on pages 94–95.

What's in this book?

In this *Success Guide*, the units are covered in the following order:

Introduction to Food-Preparation Techniques

This section covers the basic food-preparation techniques and equipment that you need to know about and will use in class.

Introduction to Cookery Processes

This section covers the different cookery processes you will use in practical work in class.

Organisation of Practical Skills

This section focuses on the skills involved in planning practical work.

Food Hygiene for the Hospitality Industry

This section covers the various aspects of food safety and hygiene and their importance to the hospitality industry.

Course assessment

The course assessment is based on a practical assignment undertaken under controlled conditions. The course assessment is set by the SQA and will:

- include a range of food-preparation techniques and cookery processes
- involve the planning and preparation of four portions of two different dishes within 1½ hours – the dishes will be either a starter and main course or a main course and dessert.

Useful information which will help you to do well in your **practical assignment** is found on pages 90–93.

Other features of the book

Top Tips

Top Tips to help you are included on each double page. These tips will

- link to the course content
- give you tips for your practical work
- give you examination tips.

Quick Tests

These are short questions which will test your knowledge. Answers are also given, but remember – don't cheat and look at them before you write your answers!

Additional Activities

This feature will provide you with a range of tasks and activities designed to apply your knowledge of the content of this book.

Leckie and Leckie Learning Lab

When you see this, it means that the activity or information is listed on the Leckie and Leckie Learning Lab page. To find these, go to www.leckieandleckie. co.uk, click on the Learning Lab button and navigate to the *Intermediate 1 Hospitality Course Notes* page.

Personal hygiene and kitchen hygiene

Throughout this course and during practical food preparation, you will be expected to follow high standards of both

- personal hygiene and
- kitchen hygiene.

Poor food hygiene can lead to outbreaks of food poisoning. The risk of contamination by micro-organisms (bacteria) can be reduced by ensuring that people handling food follow a set of hygiene rules.

Personal hygiene

It is known that the most common cause of food contamination is **people**, and therefore food-hygiene laws include rules for personal hygiene. Whether you work in the hospitality industry, study the subject at school or work in your own kitchen at home, you must follow these rules.

Hands

Hands must be kept clean at all times, particularly:

- after going to the toilet
- before handling food
- after coughing, sneezing or blowing your nose
- after touching your face, hair, nose, mouth or ears
- after touching dirty surfaces or utensils or cleaning fluids
- after handling waste food or rubbish
- before touching food that has been cooked or will not need to be cooked
- before serving, e.g. salad
- after touching raw food.

To wash your hands

You must use hot water with soap to give a good lather. Make sure between your fingers, palms, backs of hands and under your nails all receive attention. Rinse thoroughly in warm water, then dry with a disposable paper towel or a hot-air hand-dryer. Textile hand towels are not recommended due to the risk of **cross-contamination**.

Top Tip
The Food Hygiene (Scotland) Regulations 2006 deal with all the rules for a food handler. See page 79.

Top Tip
Cross-contamination is a key term which you need to learn. It means that bacteria can be passed very easily from a **contaminated source**, e.g. raw meat or hands, to an **uncontaminated food**, e.g. cooked meat.

- **Any cuts or broken skin** must be covered with a waterproof plaster, preferably blue-coloured so that it can be noticed if it falls into any food.
- **Fingernails** may harbour bacteria, so they must be kept short and clean. Nail polish or false nails can also contaminate food and should not be worn.
- **Clothing** worn in a food-handling area must be clean, must be washable and must completely cover ordinary clothing. It should be removed when visiting the toilet. Suitable footwear should be worn to prevent slipping and to protect the feet.
- **Hair** must be tied back, or suitable head-covering must be used by all food handlers. To prevent contamination of food, never comb your hair in a kitchen.
- **No jewellery** should be worn, as it harbours dirt and bacteria. Stones from the jewellery could fall into the food.
- **Strong-smelling perfume** or aftershave should not be worn, as it may taint foods.
- **Smoking**, **by law**, is not allowed in any food areas. Cigarette ash can contaminate food, while people touching mouths and coughing cause infection.
- If **people** who handle food suffer from sickness, diarrhoea, skin problems, boils or heavy colds, they must inform their supervisor or teacher, as they may contaminate food.

All food handlers should be provided with appropriate training linked to the particular job they are doing – and many businesses encourage their staff to undergo such training.

It is most important when working in the food industry that these personal-hygiene rules are strictly followed. If they are not, cross-contamination may occur, and food will become unsafe to eat.

Top Tip
Because the mouth harbours bacteria, food handlers should not eat sweets, chew gum, taste food with a finger or blow into drinking glasses to polish them.

Quick Test

1. What is the most common cause of food contamination?

2. How should hands be dried?

3. Why should jewellery not be worn by food handlers?

4. What should a food handler do if suffering from a heavy cold?

Answers 1. People **2.** Dry on disposable paper towels or hot-air hand-dryer **3.** Because it harbours dirt and bacteria, and stones could even fall into food **4.** Report it to their supervisor or teacher

Kitchen hygiene

Kitchen hygiene is linked to the environment in which food is stored, prepared and cooked.

You must always obey some simple rules to prevent possible food poisoning and to ensure good kitchen hygiene. It is a **legal requirement** that all areas where food is being prepared meet hygiene regulations.

Good kitchen hygiene is also covered in the unit **Food Hygiene for the Hospitality Industry**, e.g. food storage, types of bacteria, or design of food premises. But we will start with these simple rules.

- Always ensure that your work surfaces, equipment and utensils are clean before you start to prepare food.
- Wash chopping boards, dishes and equipment in hot soapy water after preparing each food item before going on to the next.
- Always use clean tea towels and net cloths. They should be washed at a high temperature after each use.
- Food-preparation areas should always be well ventilated and have good lighting.
- Always wash fruit and vegetables before peeling, as any unwashed fruit or vegetables can contain harmful bacteria.
- Dispose of all waste, e.g. vegetable peelings, immediately. These should be wrapped and put in a bin with a tight-fitting lid which should be emptied frequently.
- Food should always be kept COOL, CLEAN and COVERED (the three Cs) in storage to prevent contamination.

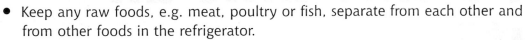

- Keep any raw foods, e.g. meat, poultry or fish, separate from each other and from other foods in the refrigerator.
- Defrost frozen foods in the refrigerator, not on the work surface in a warm kitchen.
- Use separate chopping boards for raw and cooked foods to prevent cross-contamination. It is ideal to have a specific chopping board (red) for raw meat only.
- Always store raw and high-risk foods (see page 69) in the refrigerator.
- Always use food before the 'Use by' date expires.
- Wipe up spills immediately.
- Clean equipment after use.
- Pets and other animals should never be allowed in food-preparation areas.
- Never put cooked food on any areas that raw food – meat, poultry, fish – has previously been prepared on, e.g. surfaces, chopping boards, plates etc.

Top Tip
'Clean as you go.' This means washing your dishes and cleaning your surfaces throughout your practical work.

Additional Activity

Look at the kitchen below and make a list of ten points of poor kitchen hygiene.

List what should be done to improve each point.

Quick Test

1. Before you begin to prepare food, what should be your first task?

2. What are the three Cs linked to food storage?

3. Where should you defrost frozen food?

4. What colour of chopping board should be used to prepare raw meat?

Answers 1. Ensure that work surfaces, equipment and utensils are clean 2. Cool, clean and covered 3. In the refrigerator 4. Red

What's this unit all about?

In this unit, **Introduction to Food-Preparation Techniques**, you will develop knowledge of, and skills in, basic food-preparation techniques, along with learning names of equipment and cookery terms used in practical cookery.

There are two assessments for this unit.

1. Practical exercise

This covers:

Outcome 1 – Weigh and measure foodstuffs accurately

Outcome 2 – Use a range of simple food-preparation techniques

These two outcomes are assessed together.

2. Written matching exercise

This covers:

Outcome 3 – Identify basic food-preparation equipment and cookery terms

1. Practical exercise

Let's look more closely at what you have to do to be successful.

Outcome 1: Weigh and measure foodstuffs accurately

This means you have to:

- use scales accurately to weigh foodstuffs
- use measuring jugs to measure liquids
- use measuring spoons accurately to measure foodstuffs and liquids.

Outcome 2: Use a range of simple food-preparation techniques

This means you have to:

- use a range of simple food-preparation techniques to show that the equipment is appropriate for the task
- carry out the preparation correctly and without undue waste
- maintain safe and hygienic standards throughout.

2. Written matching exercise

Outcome 3: Identify basic food-preparation equipment and cookery terms

This means you will be assessed on:

- the names and use of food-preparation equipment
- basic cookery terms.

Top Tip
It is very important to weigh and measure ingredients accurately, as your results could be spoiled as a result of using the wrong amount of ingredients.

Weighing

Scales are used to **weigh solid ingredients** such as flour, sugar and vegetables. Foods are weighed in grams or kilograms. Weighing needs to be accurate for all practical food preparation, **so do not use handy measures**. There are two main types of scales: manual scales and digital scales. Let's look at each more closely.

Manual scales

Also known as spring-balance scales.

- Manual scales have a pointer that moves along a scale to indicate the weight of food being weighed.
- They can be difficult to read.
- Some scales are designed to weigh smaller quantities of foods, and the measuring scale generally goes up in 5 g divisions.

Top Tip
1. Check that the scale pan is set onto the scales properly.
2. Check that the pointer is at '0'.
3. When checking weights, stand directly in front of the scales.

Electronic/digital scales

- Digital scales are either electronically or battery-operated.
- They have an LCD display that makes them easy to read and use.
- They can be used to measure small or large amounts of food **accurately**.
- They must always be placed on a flat surface when using.

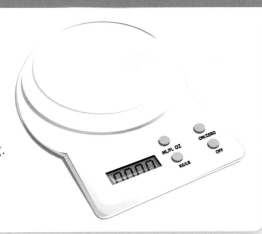

Quick Test

1. Name the two main types of scales.
2. Which type would weigh amounts of ingredients more accurately?
3. List two factors which should be checked before using manual scales.

Answers 1. Manual and digital scales **2.** Digital **3.** Check that the scale pan is set onto the scales properly; check that the pointer is at '0'; when checking weights, stand directly in front of the scales

Measuring

Liquids such as milk, water and stock are measured in units of millilitres and litres.

Measuring jugs

These are used to measure liquids.

- They are usually made from glass or clear plastic.
- Look for comfortable handles and a well-shaped pouring lip.
- They come in a range of sizes – the smallest being 250 ml.
- The measuring scale on a jug is usually shown in millilitres (ml), with the litre (L) measurements being shown on the other side of the scale.

Top Tip
1. Always place the jug on a flat surface to get an accurate measurement.
2. When checking the level of the liquid, always read the measurement at eye level.

Measuring spoons

These are used to measure small amounts of ingredients or liquids.

- They are usually made from plastic or metal.
- They can come in a variety of sizes, usually 1.25 ml, 2.5 ml, 5 ml, 10 ml and 15 ml.

Top Tip
Remember:
When measuring dry ingredients, e.g. corn flour, care should be taken to level off the dry ingredients using the back of a knife to gain an accurate measurement.

Food-preparation techniques and equipment

This section will deal with the **food-preparation techniques** you will be assessed on during your practical work and will also give you **information** about the **equipment** you will use when practising these techniques.

Throughout your practical work, it is important to work **safely**, particularly when using any sharp piece of equipment. You should follow these rules:

- When washing vegetables, always hold knives and peelers by the handle and do not leave them in the water in the bottom of the basin.
- Keep fingers out of the way when using sharp knives or graters.
- Keep the point of the knife on the chopping board.
- When carrying a knife, the blade should always point downwards.
- Do not store your knives loose in a cutlery drawer. You will blunt them, and you could give yourself a bad cut from the uncovered blades.
- Use a magnetic knife rack or a wooden knife block to store knives safely.
- Always ensure that knives and peelers are sharp – blunt equipment can be dangerous.

You will be required to be able to carry out the following techniques correctly and be able to name the equipment you use to:

- peel • cut • slice • grate • roll out • shape • pipe • mix • whisk • cream

Peel

The first technique is: Peeling. This is the process of removing the outer skin from fruit or vegetables.

Equipment required

Vegetable knife

A small knife used for trimming, peeling and shaping vegetables or cutting small food items.

Vegetable peeler

A useful tool to remove thin layers of skin from vegetables, e.g. potatoes, or firm fruits, e.g. apples.

Top Tip
Always try to peel the skin as thinly as possible. Using a vegetable peeler can be less wasteful.

Quick Test

1. Give two rules to follow to ensure that you use a measuring jug accurately.
2. Explain the technique 'peel'.
3. Which two pieces of equipment could be used to peel a potato?
4. What should you do with potato peelings?

Cut

Cutting is the process of breaking the surface of a food, to divide or make it smaller, using a sharp tool, usually a knife.

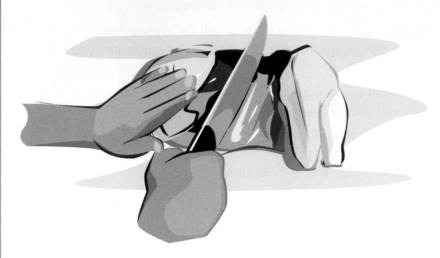

Equipment required

Cook's knife or chef's knife

Used for cutting meat, cutting and dicing vegetables. Also ideal for chopping, e.g. parsley, cabbage. This knife can vary in size from 18–25 cm. Choose the size you find most comfortable.

Vegetable knife

A smaller knife about 9–10 cm used for trimming and shaping vegetables and also for peeling or cutting small items. It is also known as a paring knife.

The following **equipment** is also required when cutting foods.

Chopping board

Colour-coded polypropylene chopping boards should be used to prevent cross-contamination of foods being prepared (see page 70).

Red – raw meat   Brown – vegetables

Blue – fish   Yellow – cooked meats

White – bakery and dairy   Green – salad and fruit

Top Tip
Remember: you will not be assessed on any technique until you have practised it a few times.

Introduction to Food-Preparation Techniques

Slice

Slicing means to cut, generally across the food item, into thin pieces that are similar in thickness. Slices usually range from 2 mm to 4 or 5 mm in thickness.

Equipment required

A cook's knife or vegetable knife.

However, an **electric food processor** can also be used to **slice** food.

An electric food processor can do many food-preparation tasks. It can blend, chop, grate, mince, purée or **slice** a range of foods. Food processors have a range of blades and attachments which carry out these different tasks very well and extremely quickly.

Top Tip
With practice, you may find that using a cook's knife will give you a better result than a vegetable knife when slicing vegetables.

Top Tip
Always switch off and unplug any electrical equipment before dismantling and cleaning.

Additional Activity

Complete the crossword below. All the answers can be found on pages 11–15.

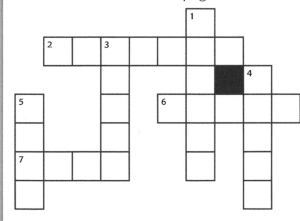

Clues

Across

2. Very accurate scales
6. A measurement of liquid
7. When peeling vegetables, remove only a thin ....

Down

1. The other name for a vegetable knife
3. The colour of chopping board used for fruit
4. An electric food processor can be used for this technique
5. You must do this to vegetables before starting to peel

Answers Across: 2. Digital **6.** Litre **7.** Skin **Down: 1.** Paring **3.** Green **4.** Grate **5.** Wash

Quick Test

1. Explain the technique 'cut'.
2. Which colour of chopping board should be used for dicing meat?
3. Describe how you would slice a cucumber.
4. What other tasks can a food processor do apart from slicing?

Answers 1. Cutting is the process of breaking the surface of a food, to divide to make it smaller, using a knife **2.** Red for raw, yellow for cooked **3.** Cut across the cucumber into thin pieces that are similar in thickness **4.** Blend, chop, grate, mince or purée

Grate

Grating is a process where rubbing solid pieces of food such as cheese or carrots against a grating instrument produces smaller pieces or shreds of that food.

Equipment required

All-purpose grater

An all-purpose grater usually has several sides, with each side having a different size of grating pattern suitable for a variety of food or purposes. Some graters are also designed with a slicing section.

It is important to use the correct side of a grater so that you get the correct size of grated food. For example, when grating cheese for a sauce the larger size of grating pattern is suitable, but if you need to grate the zest (skin) of a lemon you should use the finest side of the grater.

Rotary grater

The rotary grater is a hand-held piece of equipment that consists of a handle, a food compartment to hold what you want to grate and a cylindrical grating surface. When food is placed in the grater and the handle is turned, the grating surface rotates over the surface of the food, grating it as it moves.

This grater may also be called a **mouli grater** or **cheese grater**. It is ideal to use for grating hard or dense cheese, such as Parmesan.

Rasp grater

The rasp grater is a hand-held grater which easily moves over the food being grated. The grated food is collected either underneath or over the dish being prepared. It usually has fine grating holes and can be used for grating the zest of citrus fruit or nutmeg.

Ease of cleaning

Graters can be difficult to wash, as there are many surfaces which can trap food or dirt. This can then lead to food poisoning, as bacteria can grow in areas difficult to clean. It is important that a grater is cleaned thoroughly by brushing off any food and washing and scrubbing in very hot soapy water.

Top Tip
To save time, use a food processor if grating a large amount of ingredients.

Roll out

This is a process of making pastry or dough thinner and smoother before it is shaped.

Equipment required

Rolling pin

This is a long cylindrical utensil usually made of wood, marble or heavy plastic. It is used to roll out various types of dough.

When rolling out pastry or dough, the rolling pin and surface should be lightly floured to prevent the mixture sticking. Use a flour dredger filled with flour to sprinkle the flour evenly over the surface.

To roll out – begin to roll the dough from the centre, gently stretching it away from you. Use a 'forward, back and up' movement. Always quarter-turn the dough after each roll, as this prevents it from sticking to the surface. You should continue rolling until the dough is the thickness you require.

Flour dredger

A flour dredger is a metal or plastic container with a lid which has small holes punched in it. Do not sprinkle too much flour on your work surface, as this could make the pastry too dry and difficult to handle.

Dredgers can also be filled with caster or icing sugar which, when sprinkled on baked items, can be a quick and easy decoration.

The following **equipment** can also be used when preparing baked items:

Top Tip

Do not roll out scone mixtures, as it is easy to make the mixture too thin. Just pat the mixture flat to the required depth with the palm of your hand – remember to flour your hand lightly first!

Pastry brush

A pastry brush is a wide brush made of nylon, plastic or natural bristles and is used to glaze the top of baked items with a coating to give colour and shine, e.g. scones, bread. The coating may be milk, egg and milk, oil or a sauce.

Fish slice

A fish slice can be useful when removing large baked items from baking trays to a cooling tray, e.g. a pastry flan. It can also be used to turn food over when frying, e.g. eggs or fish. It is usually made of stainless steel and has a flexible blade.

Cooling tray

The main use for a cooling tray is to allow cooked food to be placed on it to allow the food to cool on all sides after cooking or baking. A cooling tray is similar to a metal mesh and allows the food to be cooled without falling through. The air circulates underneath the food, preventing baked foods in particular from becoming soggy.

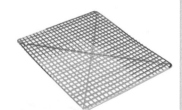

Quick Test

1. Complete the missing words in the following sentence.

   To roll out – begin to roll the dough from the _____, gently stretching it away from you. Use a _____ _____ and ____ movement.

2. What is a flour dredger used for when rolling out pastry?

3. Why should a cooling tray be used when cooling baked goods?

Shape

Shaping is the process of taking food ingredients and forming them into an appropriate shape depending on what you are making, e.g. beef burgers, shortbread, scones.

Equipment required

Shaping can be achieved in a number of ways using a variety of equipment.

Palette knife

A palette knife is a blunt-style knife used for shaping such foods as fish cakes, beef burgers or a large shortbread round. It can also be used for lifting and turning foods as well as spreading and smoothing icing on cakes.

Pastry cutters

A pastry cutter is a hand-held tool which evenly cuts shapes from pastry, biscuit or scone dough.

Plain cutters are usually used for savoury dishes while fluted cutters are used for sweet dishes.

You may also find a variety of novelty cutters such as Christmas trees, gingerbread men, or hearts.

A piping bag and tube can also be used for shaping (see page 19), for example piping choux pastry to make éclairs.

Top Tip

When using cutters, it is important to dip the cutter into flour before placing it on the dough. This will allow your shape to come loose from the cutter more easily. The cutter should be placed on the dough and pressed down firmly. This will give a sharp edge to the shape.

Pipe

This is the process of squeezing a piping bag in order to force icing or other paste-like mixture through the tip of the bag containing a piping tube for the purpose of decorating or creating special shapes.

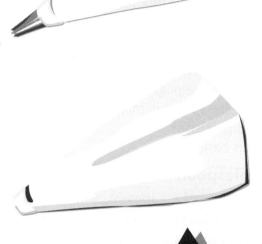

Equipment used

Piping bag

- A piping bag is a special cone-shaped bag and may be made of nylon (which is easily washed and dried) or plastic (which may also be disposable).

- To fill the piping bag, turn the top edge of the bag over your hand or over the sides of a tall measuring jug, and spoon in the mixture. Fold over or twist the piping bag to seal.

- It is always a good idea to practise a few shapes onto the sides of a plate before piping the final decoration.

- A wide variety of foods can be used for piping, e.g. whipped cream, creamed potato, biscuit dough, meringue, choux pastry for éclairs.

Tubes

- A tube will be placed into the small end of the piping bag before filling with mixture.

- The most common tubes are plain or star-shaped, with many different sizes and designs available.

- A large plain tube can be used to pipe potatoes or éclairs. Fine tubes can be used for decorative work or for writing on cakes.

- The star shape will give a very decorative finish to the ingredients you are piping. This shape, for example, can be used to decorate trifles with rosettes of cream.

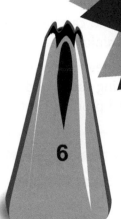

Top Tip
When piping, the pressure must come from the top of the piping bag, using one hand. The other hand, which is held in a lower position near the tube, will guide the piping bag. The piping bag must be kept upright for best results.

Quick Test

1. Explain the term 'shape'.
2. Name three different items which can be used to shape foods.
3. What are the advantages of a nylon piping bag?
4. List three uses of a plain tube.

Answers 1. Shaping is the process of taking food ingredients and forming them into an appropriate shape depending on what you are making **2.** Palette knife, pastry cutters, piping tubes **3.** They can be easily washed and dried **4.** To pipe potatoes, éclairs, decorative work, writing

Mix

This is a process of combining ingredients so that they are all distributed evenly within the mixture.

Equipment required

There are many items of kitchen equipment which can be used to **mix** ingredients.

Here are a few:

fork
spoons (metal, plastic, wooden)
whisks – see page 21
hand-held electric mixer
food processor
clean hands!

Tablespoon

This piece of equipment, while being used to **mix** ingredients, can also be used for many other purposes.

It can be used to:

- stir food together
- fold ingredients through each other
- measure dry or liquid ingredients.

The following **equipment** can be used to mix or sift dry ingredients.

Top Tip
A tablespoon is a useful measure to use for 15 ml of liquid.

Sieve

Sieves come in various sizes and can be made of plastic, stainless steel or aluminium.

A very fine mesh is used for sieving particles of dry ingredients, e.g. flour, icing sugar, and so traps air to make the finished product lighter.

Additional Activity

Create your own word search – draw 30 squares by 30 squares and fill it with as many ingredients as you can mix together. Use some of your school or college recipes or a recipe book to help you.

Whisk

This is the process of using a whisk to blend ingredients together or to incorporate air into ingredients to increase their volume, e.g. whisking egg whites, thickening cream.

Equipment used

Whisks come in different shapes and sizes, and some are used for different purposes. The whisks which are used **manually** are:

Rotary whisk

This is hand-held and turns a double whisk. It is used to beat ingredients together quickly, whisk egg whites or thicken cream, increasing their volume.

Balloon whisk

This is used for whipping light food ingredients – again increasing the amount of air in the food being whisked. It is ideal for making sauce and is used a lot by professional chefs.

Flat whisk

This whisk is ideal for beating and mixing ingredients in pans, as it bends easily to mix ingredients at the bottom or sides of a pan.

Hand-held electric whisk

These hand-held electric whisks have a range of speeds, giving you more control over the whisking/mixing process. It is ideal for sponge mixes and meringues. A food mixer can also be used for whisking.

Top Tip
When using an electric hand whisk, always start at the lowest speed and build it up gradually – this will avoid the mixture splashing out of the bowl.

Additional Activity

Complete the crossword below. All the answers can be found on pages 16–21.

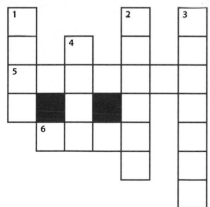

Clues

Down

1. To apply a decorative finish to a cake

2. Can also be called a mouli grater

3. Used to sprinkle flour on the table before kneading dough

4. A whisk used to mix ingredients in pans

Across

5. A knife used for shaping fish cakes

6. A type of tube used for piping

Answers Down: 1. Pipe **2.** Rotary **3.** Dredger **4.** Flat **Across: 5.** Palette **6.** Star

---

Quick Test

1. Explain the term 'mix'.

2. List four pieces of equipment with which you can mix.

3. Unjumble the following words which are all connected with whisking.

   a. Tyoarr **b.** Olbnlao **c.** Altf **d.** Nbdel
   e. Muevlo **f.** Rcetilce hkswi

Answers 1. To combine ingredients so that they are all distributed evenly within the mixture **2.** Fork, spoons, hand-held electric mixer, food processor **3. a.** Rotary **b.** Balloon **c.** Flat **d.** Blend **e.** Volume **f.** Electric whisk

Cream

This is the process of blending butter or margarine and sugar together until the mixture is light, fluffy and pale in colour due to the air being added. This process is done before adding other ingredients to make cakes, biscuits or bread doughs.

Equipment used

Wooden spoon and mixing bowl

A simple straightforward method would be to use this equipment to **cream** a mixture. It would be the easiest equipment to clean!

Hand-held electric whisk

This piece of equipment does not involve a lot of setting up and can be used quickly and efficiently to **cream** mixtures.

Always ensure that the electricity and beaters are switched off when setting it up. After using the whisk, switch off and disconnect the plug immediately. It is important to eject the beaters from the whisk for washing in hot soapy water.

Electric food processor

This piece of equipment will give extremely quick results when creaming a mixture. The food processor can also be used for many other processes such as blending, chopping, grating, mincing, puréeing and slicing a range of food ingredients. This is a very handy piece of equipment, especially if working with larger quantities of food.

> **Top Tip**
> When creaming with this equipment, have a damp net cloth under the bowl to prevent it from slipping around, **and** also ensure your butter or margarine is at room temperature to make it easier to cream.

> **Top Tip**
> Do not put any electrical appliance into water when cleaning – wipe it with a damp, soapy cloth and dry.

Quick Test

1. Complete the following description of 'creaming' using the word bank below.

   Word bank – air mixing blending soft dark salt light pale sugar heavy kneading

   Creaming is the process of _____ butter or margarine and _____ together until the mixture is _____, fluffy and _____ in colour due to the ____ being added.

2. Give a tip to use when creaming with a wooden spoon in a mixing bowl.

3. What advice would you give when setting up an electric whisk or food processor?

Additional Activities

Word search

In the word search below are 31 names of techniques and equipment that appear in this unit. Photocopy this page and see how many you can find.

A	Y	I	D	E	X	U	N	I	P	G	N	I	L	L	O	R
P	A	S	T	R	Y	B	R	U	S	H	W	D	Y	I	N	F
C	K	V	S	E	L	Z	Z	O	N	G	N	I	P	I	P	L
G	U	J	G	N	I	R	U	S	A	E	M	C	F	H	A	O
B	C	T	K	J	W	A	O	S	H	A	P	E	V	K	O	U
J	W	I	Z	M	H	C	J	L	I	M	I	X	D	N	V	R
C	H	O	P	L	J	Q	U	I	X	P	P	B	L	E	N	D
S	I	E	V	E	N	U	W	C	O	G	E	X	B	A	N	R
J	S	R	G	R	A	T	E	E	H	C	F	O	L	D	G	E
K	K	T	H	U	F	B	I	H	T	K	O	S	G	C	P	D
R	F	K	E	S	Q	Y	G	R	M	X	P	A	D	U	L	G
O	W	A	P	A	T	M	H	O	M	B	E	N	T	B	E	E
F	V	E	G	E	T	A	B	L	E	P	E	E	L	E	R	R
R	G	G	E	M	Z	I	D	L	W	Q	L	Q	Y	A	F	C
S	C	A	L	E	S	T	C	O	R	A	C	U	T	T	E	R
A	L	Z	S	S	O	D	P	U	R	E	E	Z	F	L	M	P
K	B	V	E	C	A	K	E	T	I	N	R	C	R	E	A	M

Mind Map

Draw a Mind Map to help you revise all the food-preparation techniques and equipment in this chapter. Start with the words FOOD-PREP TECHNIQUES in the centre of your page. Link each food-preparation technique to this, and then link the equipment used for each technique. An example has been given below.

FOOD PREPARATION TECHNIQUE — CREAM —

Top Tip
When mind mapping, use a different colour of pencil for each technique. Illustrate your Mind Map. This will help you remember.

Cookery terms

During your practical work and in your recipes, you will use a number of different **cookery terms.** You are expected to know what these mean.

The following **cookery terms** are the ones on which you will be assessed.

Term	Description
Bake blind	**To bake a pastry case without a filling** Baking blind is the technique cooks and chefs use to pre-cook a pastry case when the filling to be used: • needs little cooking itself, so pre-cooking the pastry shell is needed so that the pastry will not be served uncooked • is wet or a liquid – baking blind helps prevent the pastry from absorbing the moisture and becoming soggy • is dense – the pastry is baked blind to ensure that it is cooked properly.
Beat	**To add a small amount of air to a mixture using a spoon or fork** This technique, for example, is used to beat egg and milk together for a glaze so that both ingredients are mixed but not a great deal of air is added.
Blend	**To mix together a dry ingredient with a liquid to give a smooth paste** This technique is used to blend custard powder and milk together to make a smooth paste before adding warm milk.
Coat	**To cover food with a layer of egg and breadcrumbs to protect it when cooking** Foods such as fish cakes and potato croquettes are coated. The egg sets when heated and holds the breadcrumbs onto the food. This gives the food a crisp coating and helps to prevent it from falling apart during cooking.
Cream	**To mix together margarine and sugar until light and fluffy** See page 22. This technique is used in cake-making and in the making of butter icing. The finished mixture should fall easily off a wooden spoon when gently shaken.
Fold	**To gently mix one ingredient into another with a metal spoon to minimise air loss** This technique is used to add self-raising flour into a whisked sponge mixture or to add caster sugar into a meringue mixture. Folding-in is done with a figure-of-eight movement – round the outside of the bowl, and through the centre while gently turning the mixture over. This is done carefully until the ingredient added has been folded in and no air is lost.

Top Tip
Allow the pastry to 'relax' or 'rest' for at least five minutes before trimming – this prevents the pastry shrinking during baking.

Knead	**To gently handle a pastry or dough to remove cracks before rolling out or shaping**
	This technique will also add a little air to the dough, so making it lighter.
Line	**To cover the bottom and sides of a flan case with pastry**
	It is important to lift the pastry carefully when lining a flan or cake tin. This can be done in various ways, such as:
	• carefully wrapping the pastry round a rolling pin and gently placing it in the flan ring, or
	• folding the pastry in half and then into a quarter and lifting it into the flan ring. The pastry should then be gently unfolded and used to line the flan ring.
Whisk	**To increase the volume of the mixture by adding air**
	Whisking can also be used to combine ingredients together, for example whisking egg, oil and milk together when making muffins.

Quick Test

The following cookery terms have become muddled.

Try to match the correct term (A–G) with its definition (1–7).

Term	Definition
A Blanch	**1.** To add salt and pepper
B Flake	**2.** To make a smooth thick paste
C Garnish	**3.** To remove solid food from a liquid
D Glaze	**4.** To divide into small bits
E Purée	**5.** To give a shine, usually to baked foods
F Season	**6.** To dip vegetables into boiling water for a short time before quickly cooling
G Strain	**7.** To decorate a savoury dish

Copy out the chart below to help you to answer.

Term	A	B	C	D	E	F	G
Definition							

Assessment practice

To help you pass the assessment for Introduction to Food-Preparation Techniques, complete the following activities.

Look at the following recipe for Cheese and Chive Flan.

Ingredients

Pastry flan	Filling
100 g plain flour	5 ml fresh chives
pinch of salt	50 g Red Leicester cheese
50 g margarine	75 ml milk
2–3 × 15 ml water	1 egg
	salt and pepper to season

Method

1. Collect and weigh all ingredients.

2. Put on oven to Reg No 7 or 230 °C.

3. Sieve the flour and salt. Rub in the margarine until mixture resembles breadcrumbs.

4. Mix with sufficient water to make a firm dough.

5. Place a 15 cm flan ring on a baking tray.

6. Knead and roll out the pastry until it is ½ cm thick. Line the flan ring. Fork the bottom of the pastry 2 or 3 times. Leave to relax for 5 minutes. Trim edges.

7. Bake blind for 5–10 minutes until the pastry sets. Either use a strip of tin foil to support the sides or line with greaseproof paper and fill with baking beans.

8. Remove from the oven. Reduce oven to Reg No 4 or 180 °C.

9. Grate the cheese and chop the chives finely.

10. Remove the pastry case from the oven and press down gently if it has risen.

11. Whisk together the milk and egg. Add the cheese and chives to the egg mixture. Mix and pour into the pastry case.

12. Return to the oven for 20 minutes.

13. Serve on a warm plate.

1. Copy the chart shown below.

   Indicate on the chart what piece of weighing or measuring equipment would be used for the following ingredients.

Ingredients	Weighing or measuring equipment to be used
Margarine	
Water	
Flour	
Chives	
Milk	

2. Copy the chart shown below.

List the food-preparation techniques used in the recipe.

Identify the appropriate equipment which could be used for each technique.

Food-preparation techniques	Equipment which could be used for each technique in the recipe
1	
2	
3	
4	
5	
6	
7	
8	
9	
10	
11	
12	

3. For each of the following food-preparation techniques, identify the appropriate equipment you could use.

   a. Pipe **b.** Cream **c.** Whisk

4. Write out the sentences below using the words in the box – there are more words than you need!

> onions, fish slice, measure, coat, parsley, knead, beat, palette, line, tablespoon, blend, creaming

   a. A cook's knife is used to chop _ _ _ _ _ _ _.

   b. A _ _ _ _ _ _ _ _ _ is used to turn food when frying.

   c. A _ _ _ _ _ _ _ _ _ _ can be used to stir or _ _ _ _ _ _ _ .

   d. Mixing together margarine and sugar is called _ _ _ _ _ _ _ _.

   e. To _ _ _ _ means to add a small amount of air using a fork.

   f. You should _ _ _ _ food in egg and breadcrumbs to protect it when cooking.

   g. A type of knife used to shape foods is a _ _ _ _ _ _ _ knife.

   h. To _ _ _ _ is to cover the base and sides of a flan case with pastry.

Now check your answers on page 94.

What's this unit all about?

In this unit, **Introduction to Cookery Processes**, you will develop knowledge of, and skills in, a variety of cookery processes, along with learning to identify foods to use for the cookery processes.

There are two assessments for this unit.

1. Short written exercise

This covers:

Outcome 1 – Identify foods suitable for a range of cookery processes

2. Practical exercise

This covers:

Outcome 2 – Carry out the cookery processes to given specifications

Outcome 3 – Control the cookery process to minimise wastage

These two outcomes are assessed together.

1. Short written exercise

Let's look more closely at what you have to do to be successful.

Outcome 1: Identify foods suitable for a range of cookery processes

This means you will be assessed on:
- choosing two suitable foods for each of five cookery processes.

2. Practical exercise

Outcome 2: Carry out the cookery processes to given specifications

This means you will have to:
- carry out the following range of cookery methods correctly:
  Boiling   Poaching   Steaming   Stewing
  Baking   Grilling   Shallow frying
- use a variety of foods – vegetables, fruit, eggs, meat, fish, dry goods – in carrying out the cookery processes
- maintain safe and hygienic standards throughout.

Top Tip
Seven cookery processes are covered in this unit, so you must revise all of the processes and their suitable foods.

Outcome 3: Control the cookery process to minimise wastage

This means you will have to:
- regularly monitor the cookery process (watch as you are cooking that you do not overcook or undercook your food)
- use appropriate techniques to check if your food is ready
- produce an attractive, edible end product.

Methods of heat transference

Not all food requires to be cooked, for example some vegetables and fruit. Cooking food involves applying heat to it.

Why do we cook food?

1 To improve the texture and appearance of food.
2 To improve the flavour.
3 To kill harmful bacteria and so prevent food poisoning.
4 To make food easier to digest.

So, how do we transfer heat to food? In other words, how does heat travel to the food? This depends on the method of cooking we use.

Heat transference happens in three main ways:

- conduction   • convection   • radiation

Conduction

Conduction is the process of transferring heat through a hot solid surface directly onto a cold surface. Put simply – from a warmer to a cooler surface.

Conduction also takes place in liquids. An example of conduction is boiling vegetables in a pan.

Heat travels from the burner to the pan, heating up the pan and the water. The heat travels from the water to the potatoes, cooking them.

Metals are good conductors of heat, so they are used to make pans, as the heat will travel through the pan to the food and cook it.

Wood is not a good conductor of heat, so is often used for pan handles so that you do not burn your fingers.

Top Tip
Remember: you should always use wooden spoons for stirring hot liquid, as they do not heat up and burn your fingers.

Quick Test

1. Give two reasons why we cook food.
2. Name the three methods of heat transference.
3. Explain how carrots cook by boiling.

Answers 1. Any two correct answers: to improve the texture and appearance of food; to improve the flavour; to kill harmful bacteria and so prevent food poisoning; to make food easier to digest. 2. Conduction, convection and radiation 3. Heat travels from the burner to the pan, heating up the pan and the water. The heat travels from the water to the carrots, cooking them.

Convection

Convection is the process of transferring heat either through liquid, such as water or stock, or through air.

Hot water or air always rises and is replaced with cooler water or air.

This causes a constant movement or circulation of hot liquid or air.

This movement is called convection current.

Two examples of convection cooking are boiling an egg and roasting a chicken.

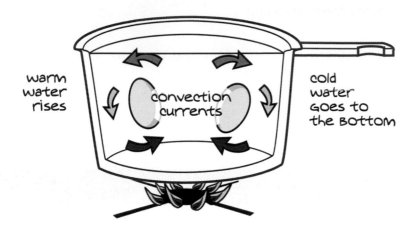

warm water rises

convection currents

cold water goes to the bottom

When boiling an egg, the boiling water circulates around the egg, transferring heat and cooking it.

When roasting a chicken, the air in the oven circulates around the chicken, the hot air rises, the cold air goes to the bottom to be heated again, and so the chicken is cooked by the convection currents.

Top Tip

If you have a fan-assisted oven, you will find the food cooks more quickly as the hot air circulates more evenly. You may need to reduce the cooking times.

Radiation

This is the direct transfer of heat onto the surface of food.

When grilling foods such as hamburgers, heat falls directly onto the surface of the food, causing it to cook. The food requires to be turned regularly so that the heat can reach both sides. Food is first of all browned under the grill on both sides to seal in the flavour and juices. After this, the heat is reduced so that the centre of the food is cooked but without burning the outside of the food.

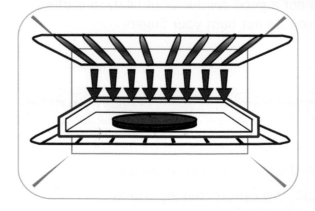

When baking a sponge:

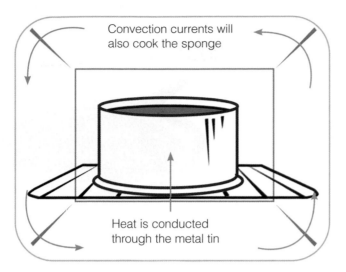

Convection currents will also cook the sponge

Heat is conducted through the metal tin

Top Tip
Remember that, in cooking most foods, more than one method of heat transference is used. There is usually a main method of heat transference as well as a secondary method of heat transference.

Cooking mediums

When we cook food, we use a cooking medium. What is a cooking medium?

- A liquid that allows heat to be transferred. Examples are water, stock, steam or oil.

Methods of cooking

Methods of cooking can be classified according to the cooking medium that is used to transfer heat.

1. Wet methods – heat is applied through water or some other liquid, and this is used to cook the food. This includes boiling, poaching, steaming and stewing.

2. Dry methods – where no liquid is used. This includes baking, grilling and shallow frying. Shallow-fat frying is a dry method of cooking, as the oil or fat does not contain water.

Quick Test

1. What is convection?
2. Explain how radiation cooks food.
3. Explain the difference between wet and dry methods of cooking.
4. What is a cooking medium?

Answers 1. Convection is the process of transferring heat either through liquid, such as water or stock, or through air. **2.** Heat falls directly onto the surface of the food, causing it to cook. **3.** Wet methods – heat is applied through water or some other liquid, and this is used to cook the food. Dry methods – no liquid is used. **4.** A liquid that allows heat to be transferred.

Boiling

Here are some important facts about boiling:

- Boiling is a wet method of cooking.
- Heat is transferred mainly by conduction, i.e. the heat from the electric ring or gas burner transfers heat through the pot to heat the liquid and then the food.
- The prepared food is cooked in a pan containing the liquid.
- The boiling action may be quick and fast – at a temperature of 100°C with bubbles all over the surface of the pan, e.g. rice or pasta

  OR

  slow and gentle, known as simmering – at a temperature of below 100°C with bubbles at one side of the pan, e.g. soup or risotto. Care should be taken to check that, during simmering, the contents of the pan are not becoming too dry.
- The liquid used may be water, stock, milk or flavoured water.

Methods of boiling

There are two ways of boiling.

1. Food is placed in cold liquid, brought to the boil and cooked, e.g. to boil eggs.

2. Food is placed in boiling liquid and cooked. This method:

- reduces the cooking time
- retains the nutritional value, e.g. vitamin C in green vegetables
- reduces the loss of colour in foods.

Advantages of boiling

- It is labour-saving and requires little attention when cooking.
- It is quite quick, and no fat is used.
- As the cooking liquid always covers the food item, there will be little shrinkage or drying out.

- It is a healthy method of cooking:
  - in the case of soups and stews, all the food is served
  - by using only enough boiling liquid to cover the food, there will be a minimal loss of nutrients.

Top Tip
During your practical work, when serving boiled foods, make sure they are well drained. Boiled rice should be served fluffed up with a fork to make it look attractive.

Suitable foods

A wide range of foods can be boiled:

- meat and poultry – silverside of beef, gammon
- fish and shellfish – lobster
- eggs and pasta – boiled egg, spaghetti, noodles
- fresh and frozen vegetables – cabbage, cauliflower, turnip, peas
- dried cereals and pulses – rice, oats, lentils

Safety points

- Choose the correct size of saucepan – if it is too small, there is a danger of boiling liquid splashing over and causing scalds.
- Position saucepan handles so that they do not stick out from the hob or become hot over the heat.
- Always move pans of boiling liquid on the hob with care.
- When lifting the saucepan lid off, lift the lid up and turn it over quickly, avoiding the steam.

Top Tip
Food items to be boiled are usually cooked in saucepans with a lid, except for rice and pasta.

Quick Test

1. Explain the difference between boiling and simmering.
2. Explain the two methods of boiling foods.
3. Name the liquids which can be used in boiling.
4. Why is boiling a healthy method of cooking?

Answers 1. Boiling – quick and fast at 100°C; simmering – slow and gentle at below 100°C. **2.** Food is placed into cold liquid. Food is placed into boiling liquid. **3.** Water, stock, milk or flavoured water. **4.** All the food is served (as in soups and stews), and by using only enough boiling liquid to cover the food there will be a minimal loss of nutrients. No fat is used.

Poaching

Here are some important facts about poaching:

- Poaching is a wet method of cooking.
- Heat is transferred mainly by conduction.
- Prepared food is cooked in milk, water, syrup or stock.
- The food is covered with the minimum quantity of liquid, then gently cooked – this is good for delicate foods such as fish or fruit.
- The food is cooked at temperatures below boiling point (at 73–93 °C) with little or no liquid movement.
- Food items to be poached are usually cooked in saucepans or in shallow-sided pans like frying pans or fish kettles (a fish kettle is specially designed for poaching whole fish, e.g. salmon).

Methods of poaching

There are two ways of poaching – shallow and deep.

1. Shallow poaching: the food is partly covered with liquid. The liquid should never be allowed to boil but should be kept at a temperature below boiling. The food should be cooked gently, covered in an oven, e.g. cuts of fish, poultry.

2. Deep poaching: the food is fully covered in the minimum amount of liquid and gently cooked. In most cases, the food is placed in the simmering water, e.g. eggs, whole fish.

Advantages of poaching

- Poaching produces dishes which are delicate in texture and full of flavour.
- It is a quick method of cooking.
- It is a healthy method of cooking, as no fat is added.
- Poached food is easy to digest, therefore suitable for invalids.
- Food that is poached will keep its shape better, as it is a gentle method of cooking, e.g. poached pears.

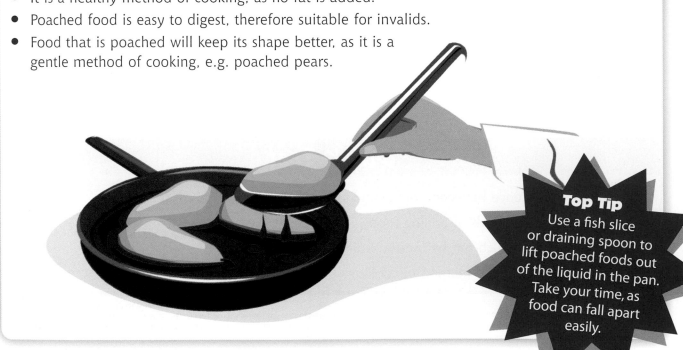

Top Tip
Use a fish slice or draining spoon to lift poached foods out of the liquid in the pan. Take your time, as food can fall apart easily.

Cookery processes: wet methods of cooking

Suitable foods

- fish and shellfish
- chicken
- eggs
- fresh and dried fruits, e.g. apricots, pears

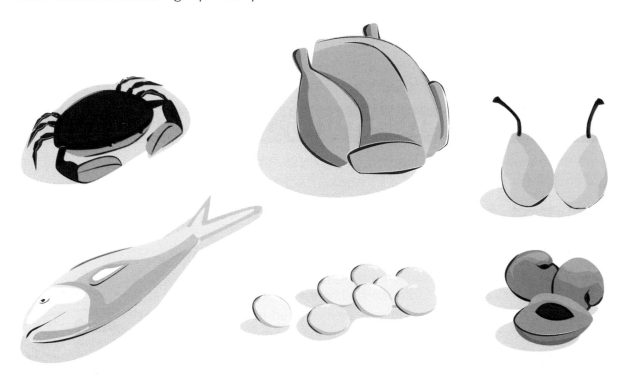

Safety points

- Choose the correct size of pan for the food to prevent spillage and possible scalding.
- Move trays and pans carefully off the hob or from the oven, as tilting may cause spillage.
- Carefully place food in the pan when adding to simmering liquid, as splashes can scald.

Top Tip
Check the cooking process regularly to see that the food is being poached and not boiled.

Quick Test

1. Unjumble the following foods suitable for poaching
   a. Lsehlihsf   b. Cicnhke   c. Osiptcra   d. Gesg
2. What type of pan would you use when poaching a whole salmon?
3. Explain the two methods of poaching.
4. Why is this method of cooking suitable for foods which you would serve to invalids?

Answers 1. a. Shellfish **b.** Chicken **c.** Apricots **d.** Eggs **2.** Fish kettle **3.** Shallow poaching, where food is partly covered with liquid and gently cooked, or deep poaching, where food is fully covered in the minimum amount of liquid and gently cooked **4.** Poached food is easy to digest

Steaming

Here are some important facts about steaming:

- Steaming is a wet method of cooking.
- Heat is transferred mainly by convection.
- Prepared food is cooked in steam rising from boiling water.
- Food may be cooked by either direct or indirect contact with the steam:
  direct – in steamer or pan of boiling water, e.g. jam sponge
  indirect – between two plates over a pan of boiling water, e.g. fish.

Methods of steaming

There are three methods of steaming foods, which use different items of equipment depending on the situation.

Plate method

Food is put on a plate or wire steamer basket and placed on top of a pot of boiling water, then totally covered with a pot lid or tin foil. This is suitable for pieces of fish, e.g. salmon, smoked haddock. Potatoes and other vegetables may be cooked in the boiling water at the same time.

Saucepan method

Water is placed in a saucepan, and the food is put in a tightly covered bowl and then placed into the boiling water. Food should be well covered to protect it from the steam and prevent it from becoming soggy.

Tiered method

This popular, economical method can be used on the hob or with an electric steamer. The advantage of an electric steamer is that food can be timed, the water does not boil dry and a whole meal can be cooked at one time.

Top Tip
Make a strong, folded strip of tin foil, about 2 cm wide, to place under and up the sides of the bowl to help lower and lift the bowl safely into and out of the boiling water.

Advantages of steaming

- No fat is added, and so food is easy to digest and will have a light texture.
- There is little loss of nutrients or flavour, as food is not in contact with water.
- It is particularly suitable for cooking vegetables; no salt is needed, as the flavour is kept.
- Food is unlikely to be overcooked or dried out and will keep its colour and texture at the same time.
- Little attention is needed while the food is cooking, except to top up the water.

Suitable foods

- fish and shellfish
- eggs
- vegetables – including potatoes
- savoury puddings, e.g. steak and kidney pudding
- sweet puddings, e.g. steamed sponge, Christmas pudding.

Safety points

- Steam is very hot. Take care when removing or checking foods.
- Boiling water should be kept handy to top up the pan if the water evaporates. Do not let the water boil dry.
- Always use oven gloves or a heavy-duty kitchen towel to lift containers which have been used in the steaming process.

Top Tip
Steaming can be a long method of cooking, and so time has to be considered when planning the serving of dishes.

Quick Test

1. Describe 'steaming'.
2. Name the three methods of steaming.
3. Why is steaming an economical method of cooking?
4. Name four suitable types of food for steaming.

Answers 1. Prepared food is cooked in steam rising from boiling water. **2.** Plate, saucepan and tiered methods **3.** As more than one food or a whole meal can be cooked at one time **4.** Fish and shellfish, eggs, vegetables/potatoes, savoury or sweet puddings

Stewing

Here are some important facts about stewing.

- Stewing is a wet method of cooking.
- Heat is transferred mainly by conduction.
- Prepared food, which is usually cut into pieces, will be cooked in the minimum amount of liquid.
- The liquid may be water, stock or a sauce.
- Both the food and the liquid in which the food is cooked are served.
- Stewing is a long, slow and more gentle cooking method, so cooking times must be considered when planning timing of meals.

Methods of stewing

- Stewed foods may be cooked in a pan with a tight-fitting lid on the hob

OR

- Stewed foods may be cooked in a covered casserole dish or pan in the oven. This method is called casseroling.

Top Tip
When serving stewed foods, make sure that a sufficient quantity of liquid is served at the same time. Your dish should not be too dry or have too much liquid.

Advantages of stewing

- Valuable nutrients will not be lost, as the food and the liquid from the stew are served together.
- It can be a healthy method of cooking, as visible fat from the meat or poultry can be trimmed off.
- Stewing is an ideal method of cooking tougher cuts of meat, poultry or game, as the meat is made very tender.
- This cookery method is economic on fuel and can be economic in labour, as food can be cooked in bulk, e.g. Bolognese sauce.
- It is an inexpensive method of cooking, as cheaper cuts of meat can be used.

Suitable foods

- fish and shellfish
- poultry and game, e.g. chicken, duck, pheasant
- fruits, e.g. apples, rhubarb, pears
- red meats, e.g. beef, mutton, lamb, pork
- vegetables, e.g. onions, tomatoes, peppers

Safety points

- Care must be taken when lifting the lid from the saucepan or casserole, as steam could badly scald.
- If the pan has been on the hob for some considerable time, the pan handle may have become hot. Use oven gloves or a thick kitchen towel to move the pan.
- Stir the stew regularly and top up with additional liquid as required. This will prevent the stew from becoming dry and will prevent possible burning.
- Stews should not be boiled, as this can make meat tough. The stew should be simmered only.

Top Tip
When reheating stews, they must be brought to the boil and then simmered for at least 15–20 minutes. Reheated foods must reach at least 82°C.

Additional Activity

Complete the crossword below. The answers are upside down.

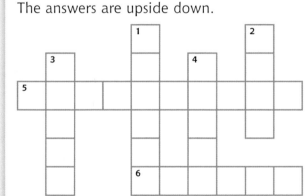

Clues

Down

1. These can be poached or stewed
2. Could be a disadvantage of stewing
3. A very gentle method of cooking for delicate foods
4. This rises from boiling water and is used to cook food

Across

5. The main method of transferring heat in wet methods of cooking
6. A gentler version of boiling

Quick Test

1. Why is stewing a healthy and nutritional method of cooking?
2. Apart from being healthy, give two other advantages of stewing.
3. What fruits are suitable for stewing?
4. Which parts of the cooker can be used for stewing?

Baking

Here are some important facts about baking.

- Baking is a dry method of cooking.
- Prepared food and food products are cooked mainly by convection in a pre-heated oven.
- Hot air circulating the oven cooks the food by direct heat, also heating whatever the food is sitting on, e.g. baking tray.
- As heat rises, the top part of the oven is hotter than the bottom part – this is the reason why food on the top shelf of the oven may cook more quickly. There is less difference in a fan-assisted oven, where the food is cooked more evenly.
- When baking, it is important that ovens are pre-heated to the correct cooking temperature so that heat is immediately applied to the product. This will take about 10 minutes. Pre-heating is important, as raising agents in bread and cakes need an instant hot temperature to work well.
- Baking trays and a wide range of ovenproof dishes are required when baking, as well as wire cooling trays on which to cool baked items.

- When making cakes and sponges, do not open the oven door until at least half the cooking time has passed, as the cold air going into the oven may make the cakes collapse.

Top Tip
If two baked items have to be cooked at the same time, the item requiring the higher temperature should be placed on the top shelf and the item requiring the cooler temperature on the lower shelf. Remember hot air rises!

Advantages of baking

- Baked food looks and tastes good. It also smells good.
- A wide range of savoury and sweet foods can be produced.
- More than one item can be cooked at one time, so saving fuel.
- Can be a healthier method of cooking, e.g. baked potatoes, apples.
- Food needs little attention when cooking.

Suitable foods

- fruit, e.g. apples, pears, peaches
- potatoes
- puddings – milk and egg custard puddings, baked rice
- flour products – cakes, bread, pastry, quiches, flans
- vegetables – tomatoes, peppers, onions
- main dishes, e.g. lasagne, shepherd's pie, ready-made meals

Safety points

- When lighting the gas oven, always ensure the door is open so that you can check the gas has ignited.
- When placing items on an oven shelf, place on the middle of the shelf to ensure that the food is evenly baked.
- Always use oven gloves when putting items into the oven and removing them from the oven.
- Ensure that your wrists and forearms are protected by oven gloves in case the baking tray slips.

Top Tip
Safe oven procedure is very important.
1. Place the baking tray on the cooker hob.
2. Open the oven door fully.
3. Using oven gloves, place the baking tray into the oven safely.

Quick Test

1. Why is it important that ovens are pre-heated when baking?

2. When is it important to use oven gloves when baking?

3. Why should you not open an oven door too soon if you are baking sponge cakes?

4. State the three actions to follow to ensure safe use of the oven.

Answers 1. Pre-heating is important because raising agents in bread and cakes need an instant hot temperature to work well. **2.** When putting items into the oven and removing them from the oven. **3.** Because the cold air going into the oven may make the cakes collapse. **4.** Place the baking tray on the cooker hob. Open the oven door fully. Using oven gloves, place the baking tray into the oven safely.

Grilling

Here are some important facts about grilling.

- Grilling is a dry method of cooking.
- Prepared food is cooked mainly by radiated heat directly from the source of heat:
  - Grilling foods **over** a heat source, which may be fired by charcoal, electricity or gas, e.g. barbecue
  - Grilling foods **under** a heat source, which may be fired by gas or electricity, e.g. grill in a cooker
  - Grilling foods **between** electrically heated grill bars, e.g. contact grill, grilling machines
- When possible, use leaner cuts of meat and trim off excess fat before cooking.
- Pre-heat grill to seal foods quickly, to give a good colour and to prevent loss of moisture and nutrients.
- Reduce heat during cooking to prevent burning the outside of the food and to make sure the centre of the food is thoroughly cooked.
- Grilled foods, e.g. steak, are served at a particular degree of cooking which depends on the type of food item being cooked and the customer's choice.

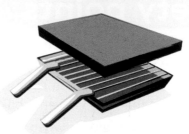

Advantages of grilling

- A very quick method of cooking which saves time and also retains the nutrients in the food.
- Fat in food melts and drips out, so grilling is a healthy method of cooking.
- Food looks attractive.

Top Tip
Some foods are better brushed lightly with oil to prevent them drying out.

Suitable foods

- good-quality cuts must be used when grilling meat, poultry and game
- offal and bacon, e.g. sliced liver, kidney and gammon steaks
- poultry and game, e.g. chicken, turkey
- fish, e.g. trout, salmon
- shellfish, e.g. large prawns and scampi
- fruit and vegetables, e.g. mushrooms, tomatoes and pineapple
- made-up items and convenience foods, e.g. burgers, sausages

Safety points

- Ensure that all grilled foods are thoroughly cooked, especially high risk foods such as chicken and pork.
- Always use oven gloves when placing the grill pan under the grill and when removing it.
- Use food tongs to turn foods over.
- When grilling, do not leave the grill unattended as the fat can spark out of some food and catch fire.

Top Tip
Most grilled foods need to be turned during cooking so that they cook evenly.

Additional Activity

The following word search contains eleven foods suitable for grilling. List them below.

J	B	U	R	G	E	R	S	P	E
X	Z	W	B	G	A	M	M	O	N
C	H	I	C	K	E	N	O	F	S
L	I	O	H	O	T	R	O	U	T
I	A	V	O	D	N	A	R	S	O
V	Y	T	P	U	M	Q	H	B	M
E	F	I	S	H	C	K	S	G	A
R	Y	E	K	R	U	T	U	R	T
N	H	K	A	E	T	S	M	L	O

Answers Tomato, Mushrooms, Fish, Chops, Burgers, Trout, Steak, Chicken, Turkey, Gammon, Liver

Quick Test

1. Explain the cookery method 'grilling'.
2. Apart from the grill on a cooker, list two other ways that food may be grilled.
3. Why is grilling called a 'healthy' method of cooking?

Answers 1. Prepared food is cooked mainly by radiated heat directly from the source of heat **2.** Barbecue, contact grill, grilling machines **3.** Fat in food melts and drips out

Shallow frying

Here are some important facts about shallow frying.

- Shallow frying is a dry method of cooking.
- Prepared food is cooked in a pre-heated pan with a small quantity of fat or oil.
- Shallow frying is a fast method of cooking because heat is conducted from the hot surface of the cooking pan directly to the food. Heat is then conducted through the food.
- Shallow frying is suitable only for certain foods that can be cooked quickly.
- The following equipment can be used for shallow frying: frying pan, electric frying pan, wok, electric wok, omelette pan, griddle pan, sauté pan
- Ensure that the presentation side of the food (the side of the food that will be uppermost when served on a plate) is fried first so that the appearance is better.

Methods of shallow frying

1. Shallow frying. This involves the cooking of food in a layer of hot fat that comes halfway up the food.
2. Dry frying. Some foods, e.g. bacon and sausages, can be fried without the addition of fat, as they contain sufficient fat to prevent them from sticking to the pan.
3. Stir frying. This is the process of cooking foods such as fish, meats or vegetables quickly at a high temperature, using as little oil as possible.

Top Tip

It is important when shallow frying to have the fat or oil at the correct temperature. If the temperature is too low, the food will absorb the fat and become greasy. If too high, the outside may brown very quickly but the inside may not be cooked.

Advantages of shallow frying

- Quick method of cooking.
- Gives flavour to food but adds extra fat unless a non-stick frying pan is used.
- Dry and stir frying are healthier methods of frying foods.

Suitable foods

- meats such as steaks, chops, cutlets, bacon
- poultry – chicken and turkey
- fish, e.g. trout, haddock
- eggs, e.g. fried egg, omelette
- vegetables, e.g. peppers, mushrooms
- fruits, e.g. bananas, peaches, apples
- batters and doughs, e.g. pancakes, crepes
- convenience foods, e.g. burgers, sausages

Safety points

- Always pre-heat the oil or fat to reduce both fat absorption into the food and the risk of the food sticking to the pan.
- Place the foods with the longest cooking times into the pan first so that they are thoroughly cooked.
- Foods which are shallow fried need to be carefully turned to ensure even cooking.
- When shallow frying, do not leave the pan unattended, as the fat could catch fire.
- If the fat does catch fire, then you should cover the pan with a tight-fitting lid, damp tea towel or fire blanket to exclude the oxygen.

  Leave it to cool before moving it.

  Call the fire brigade if the fire gets out of control.

Top Tip
Never soak the frying pan immediately after you have finished using it – the water will spurt and may scald you. Leave it to cool before soaking.

Additional Activity – revision cards

Play a game of matching cards using the information in this *Success Guide*.

Cut 21 pieces of card or paper approximately 10 cm by 10 cm.

Write a method of cooking on each of 7 pieces of card – check this on page 28.

On another 7 pieces of card, write an advantage of each method of cooking.

On the remaining 7 pieces of card, write two foods suitable for each method of cooking.

Mix the advantages and suitable foods as you would do with a pack of cards.

Set out the methods of cooking cards on your desk, and match each one with the correct advantage and suitable foods.

As a way of revising, you could do this with other areas of the course content, e.g. tests for readiness, hygiene etc.

Quick Test

1. How is heat transferred in shallow frying?
2. Why should oil be at the correct temperature when starting to shallow fry?
3. Unjumble the following types of pan which can be used for shallow frying.
   a. Nygfri   b. Temlteoe   c. Okw   d. Dregldi
4. What is stir frying?

Answers 1. Conduction **2.** If the temperature is too low, the food will absorb the fat and become greasy **3. a.** Frying **b.** Omelette **c.** Wok **d.** Griddle **4.** This is the process of cooking foods such as fish, meats or vegetables quickly using as little oil as possible

Testing for readiness

During your practical activities, you will have used a variety of foods: vegetables, fruit, eggs, meat, fish and dry goods. It is important that you know when your food is ready, thoroughly cooked and therefore safe to eat. In the hospitality industry, the reputation of a restaurant rests on serving food that is edible and correctly cooked.

Vegetables

Root vegetables, such as potatoes and turnips, are cooked when:

- they can be easily pierced with a fork and feel soft when firm pressure is applied.

Other vegetables which grow above ground, such as broccoli and cauliflower, are cooked when:

- they resist slightly when pierced with a fork. They should be tender but still be crisp when served.

Fruit

Fruits such as apples and pears are cooked when:

- they can be easily pierced with a fork or skewer and feel soft when firm pressure is applied.

Eggs

Depending on the method, eggs are cooked when:

- both the yolk and white are not liquid. The yolk can be softer than the white, e.g. in a soft boiled or poached egg.

Top Tip
Remember to check the clock when starting to cook your dishes for any cookery process. Timing is important to prevent either overcooking or undercooking.

Meat

Generally, meats are cooked when:

- no pink 'juices' are seen running out when the meat is tested with a skewer. A food temperature probe can be used to check the internal temperature of large pieces of meat to ensure that the centre of the food is sufficiently hot.

Chicken

Cook until the internal temperature reached is between 80 and 85 °C. Use a skewer to pierce the thigh of a whole chicken; when juices run clear and not pink, the chicken is cooked.

Pork

Cook until the internal temperature reached is between 80 and 85 °C. All juices should be clear when tested.

Beef

Cook until the internal temperature reached is between 63 and 65 °C. Beef can be cooked 'rare', i.e. it will have pink juices flowing – this depends on personal tastes.

Fish

Fish is cooked when:

- you are able to easily insert the tip of a thin-bladed knife or skewer into the thickest part of the fish
- the fish appears white in colour or opaque
- the flesh of the fish can easily 'flake' or come away from the bone of the fish.

Dry goods

Rice

- Rice can be tested by carefully eating a small rice grain – it should not feel grainy or hard.
- The rice can also be tested by gently squeezing a grain between your fingers – it should not feel grainy.
- The rice looks slightly swollen and fluffy.

Long-grain white rice should be cooked in boiling salted water for 12 minutes.

Long-grain brown rice should be cooked in boiling salted water for 20–25 minutes.

Top Tip
The time for cooking rice will depend on the type chosen.

Pasta

- Pasta is cooked to the stage known as 'al dente', meaning that there should be a slight firmness or bite to it when you taste it.
- It looks slightly swollen with water.

Remember that you can buy quick-cook pastas which will require a much-reduced cooking time. Check the label before using.

Cake mixture

Cake mixture is ready when:

- a warmed skewer is inserted into the centre of a fruit cake; if it comes out clean, the cake is ready.
- a sponge cake is golden brown, well risen and springy to touch. The mixture should have shrunk away slightly from the edge of the tin.

Pastry

Pastry is ready when:

- the base of the pastry is firm and the pastry is golden brown.

Scone mixture

Scone mixture is ready when:

- the scone is well risen and golden brown.

Quick Test

1. How would you test to see if potatoes were ready?
2. Should any juice coming out of a cooked chicken be clear or pink?
3. What does the term 'al dente' mean?
4. How would you test to see if a fruit cake was cooked?

Answers 1. They can be easily pierced with a fork and feel soft when firm pressure is applied **2.** Clear **3.** There should be a slight firmness or bite to it when tasted **4.** A warmed skewer is inserted into the centre of a fruit cake; if it comes out clean, the cake is ready

Assessment practice

To help you pass the assessment for Introduction to Cookery Processes, complete the following activities.

1. a. The word search below contains a selection of foods you may have used for each cookery process. You will find all the answers on pages 32–45.

Z	R	S	T	O	C	I	R	P	A	P	S
Q	M	C	P	L	F	P	R	I	C	E	F
H	T	O	M	A	T	O	E	S	H	E	U
K	K	N	D	S	C	T	G	U	I	G	E
E	X	E	G	O	E	A	V	I	C	N	C
F	I	S	H	W	S	T	E	A	K	O	B
J	A	R	A	E	H	O	U	Y	E	P	J
T	G	N	L	I	A	E	B	R	N	S	V
X	D	P	E	G	G	S	C	K	N	D	T
J	P	Q	F	H	L	W	N	I	Y	I	O
A	T	S	A	P	Z	M	B	K	R	O	P

Answers Pasta, pork, eggs, sponge, steak, fish, apricots, tomatoes, rice, chicken, scones, turnip, potatoes, apple

b. Try to match each food to a cookery process – remember that some foods are suitable for more than one cookery process.

c. Copy out and complete the chart below – this will give you a hint of how many foods you should find suitable for each process.

Cookery process	Suitable foods	Number of foods suitable for each process
Boiling		6
Poaching		5
Steaming		5
Stewing		8
Baking		10
Grilling		5
Shallow frying		9

48

2. During your practical, you will have had to monitor each cookery process and test your dishes for readiness. These questions will help you during your practical assessments to decide whether your food is correctly cooked.

a. Explain the difference between boiling and simmering.

b. What is the temperature used when poaching foods, and how does this benefit foods?

c. Why should steamed foods be well covered?

d. Why should stews be simmered?

e. Describe the safe way to place a baking tray in the oven.

f. After sealing foods quickly at the start of grilling, why should the heat be reduced?

g. What should you do if the fat catches fire during shallow frying?

h. Copy the chart shown below.

Explain how you would test to see if each of the following foods is ready.

Food	Test for readiness
Boiled potatoes	
Poached pears	
Steamed broccoli	
Boiled pasta	
Baked sponge flan	
A whole roast chicken	
Grilled fish	
Boiled rice	
Baked fruit cake	
Apple pie	

Now check your answers on page 94.

What's this unit all about?

This unit, **Organisation of Practical Skills**, is particularly important, as it will help you achieve a good award in your practical assignment for Intermediate 1 Hospitality: Practical Cookery.

The key to success is effective planning and organisation of your practical work, whether in your kitchen at home or school, or in a professional kitchen.

Effective planning will make you:

- confident
- prepared for work
- more aware of how to manage your time
- able to cope even when things go wrong
- enjoy what you are doing
- less stressed.

This unit will help you to build up your written planning skills, as well as your practical and organisational skills, by completing a number of different practical exercises safely and hygienically.

The practical exercise will link to a different situation, for which you have to choose suitable tasks or recipes.

The assessment for this unit is a practical exercise which will cover all of the following four outcomes:

Outcome 1 – Preparing for a task or tasks (requiring a minimum of five components and at least eight processes in their production)

Outcome 2 – Prepare a plan of work for the chosen task

Outcome 3 – Carry out the task to achieve the desired outcome

Top Tip
Try to practise your written planning skills for as many different practical exercises as possible – this will give you confidence

Outcome 1 – Preparing for a task or tasks

This means you have to:

- **Choose** a recipe or recipes suitable for the task.

  Each recipe has to:

  – include at least five ingredients (known as components)

  – use eight cookery processes – these can be either food-preparation techniques and/or cookery processes.

To help you choose your processes, look at the list below. These are the ones you have used in:

- Introduction to Food-Preparation Techniques
- Introduction to Cookery Processes
- **Requisition** all your resources. This means you should order:

  – all food ingredients

  – any special equipment, e.g. electric hand blender, plain flan rings

  – any other resources, e.g. baking parchment, tin foil.

Top Tip
Remember: a task is a piece of work to be undertaken or completed, e.g. a practical exercise.

Top Tip
Most food ingredients must be ordered in accurate METRIC measurements – grams and millilitres. Some ingredients may be ordered in units, e.g. ½ stock cube.

Introduction to Food-Preparation Techniques	Introduction to Cookery Processes
Peel Cut Slice Grate Roll out Shape Pipe Mix Whisk Cream Weigh Measure Sieve Bake blind Beat Knead Fold Blend Line Coat Chop	Boiling Stewing Poaching Steaming Grilling Baking Shallow frying
In addition, you may also have used:	**In addition, you may also have used:**
Trim Melt Purée Chop Dice	Sauté Simmering Stir frying Microwaving

Quick Test

1. Give two reasons why it is important to plan.
2. What does the term 'requisition' mean?
3. What three resources should be included in a requisition?
4. What type of measurement should be used to order solids and liquids?

Outcome 2 – Prepare a plan of work for the chosen task

This means you have to:

- **Plan** how you are going to carry out your task in a logical order in the time you have been given.

You need to consider the following:

Start time – 2 pm

Finish time – 3 pm

and what you are going to do within this time allocation.

'Think smart' and include the following areas in your plan of work:

- personal-hygiene preparation – remove jewellery, clean apron, cover or tie back hair, wash hands
- collecting equipment
- collecting ingredients
- timings for the following activities:
  - pre-heating of oven, turn oven off
  - preparation of ingredients
  - cooking times, testing for readiness
  - refrigeration if your dish has to be served cold
  - washing up. Remember to 'clean as you go'. This stops a pile of dirty dishes building up!
  - warming of serving dishes
  - taste for seasoning
  - presentation: garnishing and decoration

You need to complete a **plan of work**. It will look like this.

Times	Sequence of work	Notes
Times: – *are normally allocated in blocks of 5 minutes – this will depend on the task* – *try to divide your task into easily identified stages* – *these stages will combine a number of processes*	Activities will include: – *most of the activities listed above* – *all the stages of the recipe: preparation, cooking and serving*	Notes could include: – *oven temperatures* – *the finishing times of cookery processes*

Top Tip
During practical lessons, try to become aware of how long you are spending on preparation techniques such as chopping. This will help you to plan your time better.

On pages 55 and 57, there are examples of completed plans of work.

Your teacher will assess Outcomes 3 and 4 together.

Outcome 3 – Carry out the task to achieve the desired outcome

This means you have to:

- Complete the task you have chosen within the time.
- Follow the recipe correctly.
- Show a high standard of practical skills and use the correct techniques and processes throughout.
- Present the task in the quantity or portion size required.
- Present the task in a commercially acceptable condition. This is very important when you serve your dishes. The following should be taken into account:
  - serve hot dishes hot, cold dishes cold
  - dish should be clean.

Top Tip
Try to taste your dish before serving, if possible – you will gain marks in the final practical assignment if your dish is tasty.

Outcome 4 – Use safe working practices

This means you have to:

- Wear appropriate clothing
  - cool, clean clothing
  - sensible shoes
  - clean apron or overall
- Keep a clean and tidy work area
  - dispose of vegetable peelings or any waste as soon as possible
  - good personal and kitchen hygiene
  - 'clean as you go'
- Use the equipment safely
  - take care with knives and sharp equipment such as graters
  - follow instructions to use electrical equipment safely and with confidence.

Quick Test

1. What personal-hygiene preparations should be carried out before starting a practical task?
2. Describe what 'appropriate clothing' means in a practical food-preparation class.
3. Why is 'clean as you go' important?

Answers 1. Remove jewellery, clean apron, cover or tie back hair, wash hands **2.** Cool, clean clothing, sensible shoes, clean apron or overall **3.** Stops dirty dishes building up

Sample practical exercises

Practical exercise 1

You have been given the following task: **Plan and prepare a savoury flan for a friend.**

Outcome 1 – Preparing for a task or tasks

- Choose a suitable recipe. Each recipe has to:
  - include at least five ingredients (known as components)
  - use eight cookery processes – these can be food-preparation techniques and/or cookery processes.

You have decided to make **Cheese and Chive Flan – see page 26 for the recipe.**

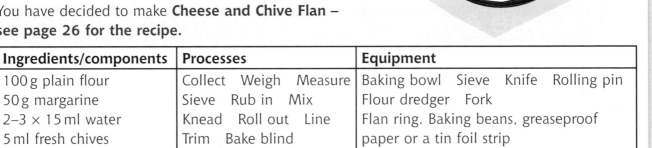

Ingredients/components	Processes	Equipment
100 g plain flour 50 g margarine 2–3 × 15 ml water 5 ml fresh chives 50 g Red Leicester cheese 75 ml milk 1 egg salt and pepper	Collect Weigh Measure Sieve Rub in Mix Knead Roll out Line Trim Bake blind Grate Chop Whisk Bake	Baking bowl Sieve Knife Rolling pin Flour dredger Fork Flan ring. Baking beans, greaseproof paper or a tin foil strip Measuring spoons – 5 ml, 15 ml Measuring jug Baking tray Grater Scissors or cook's knife Whisk Serving dish Oven gloves

As you can see:
- More than five ingredients/components will be used
- More than eight processes will be used.

The next stage will be to complete a **food requisition sheet.** Copy the one below (or one downloaded from the Learning Lab section of Leckie and Leckie's website).

Remember to include all the ingredients you will need and any other specialist pieces of equipment you may need to order.

Top Tip
Use the information in the ingredients/component column above to help you complete the requisition sheet.

FOOD REQUISITION SHEET
Name .... Class .... Teacher .... Date required ....
Name of item ....

	Quantity		Quantity
Meat/poultry		Vegetables	
Fish		Fruit	
Dairy		Dry stores	
Other equipment/resources required			

Outcome 2 – Prepare a plan of work for the chosen task

This means you have to:

• Plan how you are going to carry out your task in a logical order in the time you have been given.

This is an example of a time plan for making the Cheese and Chive Flan in **60 minutes**.

Times	Sequence of work	Notes
9:00–9:05 am 9:05–9:20 am	Personal-hygiene preparation: put on apron, remove jewellery, cover or tie hair back, wash hands. Put on oven at Reg No 7 or 230 °C. Collect equipment and ingredients for the pastry. Make the pastry. Line the flan ring, and leave pastry to relax for 5 minutes. Grate cheese.	9:25 am – trim pastry
9:20–9:30 am	Chop chives. Trim pastry. Bake blind for 5 minutes. Prepare egg-and-milk mixture. Test the pastry for readiness and remove from oven.	
9:30–9:35 am	Reduce oven temperature. Place serving dish to heat. Assemble flan. Place in oven for 20 minutes.	
9:35–10:00 am	Wash and tidy up unit. Serve on a warm plate at 9:55/10 am. Finish tidying up.	

Top Tip
Sometimes when planning your work, you have to work backwards from the serving time, e.g. you may have to decide the latest possible time for your dish to go in the oven so that it is thoroughly cooked.

Outcomes 3 and 4 – Carry out the task and use safe working practices

Remember that your teacher will observe and assess you while you are working.

As your planning and practical skills progress, you may have the opportunity to prepare two dishes in a longer period of time. This will give you practice for your final SQA assignment.

Quick Test

1. What would be the least amount of ingredients and processes you would require to complete a practical exercise?

2. What is the other name for ingredients?

3. What should you include in the food requisition sheet?

Answers 1. 5 ingredients, 8 processes **2.** Components **3.** All the ingredients you will need and any other special pieces of equipment you may need to order

Practical exercise 2

For your practical exercise, you have been given the following task:

Plan and prepare a two-course meal suitable for a friend who does not eat meat.

In addition to making the Cheese and Chive Flan, you have chosen to make Vegetable Soup in 90 minutes.

Vegetable Soup

Ingredients

100 g onions	1 litre water
300 g carrots	2 vegetable stock cubes
150 g turnip	Pinch of dried mixed herbs
10 ml olive oil	5 ml parsley

salt and pepper to taste

Method

1. Wash vegetables, peel and rewash.

2. Chop into even-sized pieces.

3. Gently fry (sauté) the vegetables in the olive oil in a covered pan for 5 minutes until tender. Do not colour.

4. Add the water, dried mixed herbs, stock cubes and seasoning. Bring to the boil, and simmer for 20 minutes.

5. Wash the parsley in a sieve. Dry carefully in absorbent paper. Chop.

6. Skim off any fat from the soup, taking care not to remove too much of the liquid.

7. Remove from the heat and allow to cool.

8. Purée the soup in a liquidiser or a food processor, or with a hand blender.

9. Stir in the parsley and taste for seasoning. Reheat.

10. Serve in a clean, hot tureen or bowl.

Top Tip
Planning for two dishes may mean that you have to 'dovetail' or fit together certain parts of the methods of both recipes to make better use of the time.

Outcome 1 – Preparing for a task or tasks

Remember you would have added the ingredients, processes and equipment for the Vegetable Soup to the chart along with the Cheese and Chive Flan.

Check your work against the answers opposite.

Ingredients/components	Processes	Equipment

Ingredients/components	Processes	Equipment
100 g onions	Collect Weigh Measure Wash Peel Chop	Chopping board
300 g carrots	Sauté Boil Simmer	Vegetable knife
150 g turnip	Skim Stir	Cook's knife
10 ml olive oil	Purée	Wooden spoon
1 litre water	Reheat	Pan and lid
2 vegetable stock cubes		Measuring jug
Pinch of dried mixed herbs		Scales
5 ml parsley		Measuring spoons – 5 ml, 10 ml
salt and pepper		Pot stand
		Sieve
		Tablespoon Teaspoon
		Absorbent paper
		Liquidiser, food processor or hand blender
		Tureen or bowl

As you can see:

- More than five ingredients/components will be used
- More than eight processes will be used.

The next stage will be to complete a **food requisition sheet.**

This is an example of a time plan for making Vegetable Soup and Cheese and Chive Flan in 90 minutes.

Times	Sequence of work	Notes
9:00–9:05 am	Personal-hygiene preparation: put on apron, remove jewellery, cover or tie hair back, wash hands. Put on oven at Reg No 7 or 230 °C.	
9:05–9:15 am	Collect ingredients for the soup. Prepare vegetables and chop into even-sized pieces.	
9:15–9:25 am	Sauté vegetables, add liquid to soup. Bring to the boil and simmer for 20 minutes. Wash and dry the parsley while waiting for soup to boil.	9:45 am – soup simmered until this time
9:25–9:40 am	Collect equipment and ingredients for the pastry. Make the pastry. Line the flan ring, and leave pastry to relax for 5 minutes. Grate cheese.	9:45 am – trim pastry
9:40–9:55 am	Chop chives. Trim pastry. Bake blind for 5 minutes. Skim soup and leave to cool. Prepare egg-and-milk mixture. Test the pastry for readiness and remove from oven.	9:50–9:55 am – check pastry
9:55–10:05 am	Assemble flan and put in to bake for 20 minutes. Warm serving dishes. Wash dishes. Chop parsley.	
10:05–10:15 am	Liquidise soup, add parsley, season and reheat. Serve soup in warm serving dish.	
10:15–10:25 am	Wash and dry dishes. Tidy up.	Ready at 10:20 am
10:25–10:30 am	Test flan for readiness. Serve flan on warm serving dish. Final tidy-up and finish.	

Top Tip
In class, try to serve your two dishes in the order of eating. In the SQA assignment, you will be given set times to serve each dish.

Assessment practice

To help you pass the assessment for Organisation of Practical Skills, complete the following activities:

1. Study the recipe below for *Muesli Biscuits*.

Ingredients

25 g sultanas

50 g oatmeal

75 g wheat flakes

100 g margarine

75 g demerara sugar

Method

1. Put on oven at Reg No 5, 190 °C.
2. Weigh the sultanas, oatmeal, wheat flakes and demerara sugar. Mix together in baking bowl.
3. Place the margarine into a pan.
4. Grease a Swiss roll tin with margarine.
5. Melt the margarine.
6. Add the melted margarine to the bowl and mix well using a wooden spoon.
7. Spoon the mixture into greased Swiss roll tin and press down smoothly using the back of a tablespoon.
8. Bake for 15 minutes.
9. Cut into 12 pieces while still warm.
10. Leave to cool.

    a. List the component parts.

    b. How many processes does this recipe have?

2. Using a blank requisition sheet similar to the one on page 54 (or one downloaded from the Learning Lab section of the Leckie and Leckie website), place the ingredients, specialist equipment and resources into the correct sections for each of the recipes below:

Recipe: Potato, Ham and Leek Soup

450 g potatoes	½ ham stock cube
150 g leek	2·5 ml salt
50 g onion	pinch pepper
75 g back bacon	Hand blender
500 ml water	Meat scissors
50 ml low-fat cream	

Recipe: Spicy Chicken Pasta

100 g cooked chicken	15 ml plain flour
50 g onion	150 ml water
75 g pasta shells	½ chicken stock cube
25 g sultanas	15 ml chutney
25 g frozen peas	12.5 g margarine
25 g tinned sweetcorn	15 ml low-fat yoghurt
10 ml curry powder	Garlic crusher
2.5 ml ground ginger	1 clove of garlic

Now check your answers on page 95.

Practical exercises

Top Tip
Try to choose recipes, using either your school recipes or recipes from home, that use a range of techniques and processes to give you practice in preparing plans of work. Check the Leckie and Leckie Learning Lab for some additional recipes to use.

Here is a selection of sample practical exercises that could give you practice in **preparing plans of work.** Try to prepare some of them in class time or at home to see if your planning is improving.

1. You are trying to encourage your five-year-old sister to eat more vegetables. Plan and prepare an item containing vegetables that would appeal to her.

2. Plan and prepare some suitable picnic-food items.

3. You have a friend staying overnight at the weekend. Plan and prepare a savoury dish which could be prepared in advance and then reheated in a microwave.

4. Plan and prepare a dish (or dishes) for a family meal.

5. Your school is trying to raise money for charity. As you are a Hospitality student, you have been asked to contribute to the cake stall. Plan and prepare some suitable items. (Try to make them healthy!)

6. Plan and prepare an international dish (or dishes) which could be sold in the school canteen.

7. You are going to be taking part in a swimming gala after school. Plan and prepare a lunch dish or dishes which would be filling and give you energy for your sports activity.

8. Plan and prepare a dish (or dishes) suitable for serving on a cold winter's day.

9. Your aunt, who is trying to lose weight, is coming for an evening meal. Plan and prepare a suitable main course and dessert.

10. Your brother is bringing a friend home after playing rugby. Plan and prepare a soup and main course which would be healthy and filling.

What's this unit all about?

In this unit, **Food Hygiene for the Hospitality Industry**, you will develop knowledge and skills required to maintain the safety of food throughout the production process.

Let's look more closely at what you have to do to be successful.

There are two assessments for this unit:

1. Written exercise

This is in the form of

- A case study which requires short answers and multiple-choice questions.

This assessment covers:

Outcome 1 – Identify the dangers and effects of contamination of food during two practical lessons

This means you will learn about and be assessed on

- what happens when food is contaminated
- food contamination by micro-organisms
- conditions for growth of bacteria
- types of food-poisoning bacteria
- how food can be physically contaminated
- the ways in which food can be preserved.

Outcome 2 – Identify unhygienic practices, including food-handling practices, which affect food or can lead to food poisoning

This means you will learn about and be assessed on

- personal and kitchen hygiene
- ways in which storage, preparation and serving can contaminate food.
- the law and food safety

Outcome 3 – Identify how effective design of premises and equipment is important to facilitate good hygiene practices and to conform to the law

This means you will learn about and be assessed on

- design of food premises and equipment
- cleaning effectively to prevent pests from entering food premises.

Top Tip
In this unit, you will learn lots of new words related to food hygiene. Look at page 83 'Key terms in food hygiene' to find out what these words mean.

2. Practical exercise

This assessment covers:

Outcome 4 – Demonstrate appropriate personal hygiene and food-handling practices during practical situations

This means you will be assessed on

- personal and kitchen hygiene practices.

Top Tip
You will be assessed during any two practical lessons. Your teacher will tell you when this is going to happen.

What is food poisoning?

Food poisoning is an illness caused by eating contaminated or poisonous food. It usually occurs within 1 to 36 hours after eating the food.

Symptoms usually last from 1 to 7 days and may include:

- stomach pain
- nausea
- tiredness
- diarrhoea
- fever
- dehydration
- vomiting
- headache.

The Royal Environmental Health Institute of Scotland (REHIS) has urged Scots to improve food hygiene standards to tackle what it calls the 'annual food-poisoning epidemic'. In 2006, 7335 cases were reported, which shows an increase of over 2.5 per cent compared to the previous year. However, it is also estimated that ten times as many cases are not reported – making it 200 cases every day!

The people most at risk are:

- the elderly
- young children
- pregnant women
- people who are already ill or convalescing.

Many of these people will be extremely ill, and some may die, as they have great difficulty in fighting the illness caused by food poisoning.

Within the hospitality industry, it is essential to have extremely high standards of both personal hygiene (for the food worker) and kitchen hygiene (for the working environment) to ensure that all food served is safe to eat.

Top Tip
These standards also apply to every home, Home Economics department and College kitchen.

The cost of poor hygiene can be high:

- food-poisoning outbreaks and sometimes death
- wasted food due to spoilage
- high staff turnover
- possible legal action and fines
- loss of business.

However, the benefits of high standards of hygiene in the industry are:

- food that is safe to eat
- happy and motivated staff
- reduced food wastage
- good reputation
- increased profits.

Quick Test

1. What is food poisoning?
2. Name two symptoms of food poisoning.
3. What groups of people are most at risk of food poisoning?
4. List 3 benefits of having a high standard of food hygiene to the hospitality industry.

Answers 1. An illness caused by eating contaminated or poisonous food **2.** Stomach pain, diarrhoea, vomiting, nausea, fever, dehydration, headache and tiredness **3.** The elderly, young children, pregnant women and people who are already ill or convalescing **4.** Any 3 of 5 listed

Food contamination

Food spoilage is the term used to describe the process that results in food becoming unfit for human consumption. It is caused by the action of enzymes and micro-organisms.

Enzymes

These are chemicals that are naturally found in food. They have important uses in food, although they can cause food to go bad in the following ways:

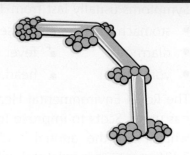

- they cause fruits and vegetables to ripen until they become inedible, e.g. bananas
- they react with air and cause foods to discolour, e.g. sliced apples.

Micro-organisms

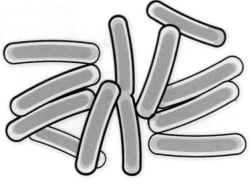

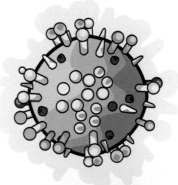

These are tiny living cells that can only be seen under a microscope. Most micro-organisms are perfectly harmless, but some can cause illness through food consumption, and others cause food spoilage. There are four main types:

- yeasts
- moulds
- bacteria
- viruses.

Top Tip
Bacteria are very small; approximately 1 000 000 could cover a pin head, so always wash your work surface with hot soapy water before starting your practical work.

Yeasts

These are made up of a single cell, which can be found in the air, in the soil or on the surface of some fruits. Jams and meats can be affected by yeasts, which can change the taste. Yeasts are used in the production of bread and wine. Heat will kill yeasts.

Moulds

Moulds are single cells and are a sort of fungus that can be seen, e.g. a blue/green 'fur' or orange spots on food. They produce spores which are carried in air and grow on the surface of foods such as bread, jam, fruit and cheese. Certain moulds produce toxins (poisons), so it is important that food that has gone mouldy should be thrown out.

Bacteria

Bacteria are single-celled organisms which we cannot see. They are found in the air, in the soil and on our bodies. Some bacteria are useful to us, e.g. in cheese-making. Others can cause food spoilage which causes changes in the appearance of the food itself, e.g. fish can become slimy and have an unpleasant smell. The food affected should be thrown out.

Others are called pathogenic bacteria. These are invisible and cause illness. Some bacteria produce **spores.** A spore is a resting phase of bacteria (where they do not multiply), protecting them against conditions such as high temperature and freezing. When conditions become more favourable, the spores release the bacteria, which then start to multiply.

Top Tip

It is not always obvious that food has been spoiled by its colour, flavour or texture.
If in doubt –
THROW OUT.

Viruses

These are extremely small pathogenic micro-organisms, which cause viral food poisoning. They get into the body through food which has not been cooked properly or has been handled after cooking by a person who is a carrier of the virus.

Quick Test

1. What is food spoilage?
2. Give two examples of how enzymes can cause food to 'go off'.
3. Name four types of micro-organisms which can cause food poisoning.
4. What is a spore?

Answers 1. The process that results in food becoming unfit for human consumption. **2.** It causes fruits and vegetables to ripen until they become inedible. e.g. bananas. They react with air and cause foods to discolour, e.g. sliced apples. **3.** Yeasts, moulds, bacteria and viruses. **4.** A spore is a resting phase of bacteria.

Main types of food-spoiling bacteria

Bacteria exist everywhere, including in and on humans, and in food, water, soil and the air. It is essential that all people involved in a food business observe good hygiene practices to prevent food poisoning.

Although bacteria are microscopic organisms, as you will see, they have different sizes and shapes.

Top Tip
Food poisoning is caused by:
Bacteria – a large number of bacteria multiply in the food
Food-borne diseases – only a few bacteria are present, and they do not need to multiply within the food.

Food-poisoning bacteria

	Sources	Symptoms	Methods of prevention	Other information
Salmonella	Raw food, e.g. meat, poultry, cheese, eggs, unpasteurised milk.	Stomach pain Diarrhoea Vomiting Fever	Good personal hygiene. Separate work areas for raw and cooked foods. Defrost poultry thoroughly. Thorough cooking of food. Refrigerated storage. Good pest control.	*Salmonella* is one of the most common causes of food poisoning in the UK.
Clostridium perfringens	Animal and human excreta. Soil on vegetables. Meat and poultry. Flies and insects. Sauces, gravies, pies.	Stomach pain Diarrhoea	Good personal hygiene. Good hygiene practices in the kitchen. Separation of raw and high-risk foods. Thorough cooking of food. Rapid cooling. Careful washing of vegetables.	Vomiting is rare. Responsible for less than 5% of the reported cases of food poisoning.

	Sources	Symptoms	Methods of prevention	Other information
Staphylococcus aureus	Human nose, mouth, skin, cuts and boils. Raw milk from cows and goats. Contaminated moist protein foods – milk, cream, cooked meats, eggs and fish products.	Stomach pain Vomiting (severe) Fever	Good personal hygiene. Use of waterproof dressings to cover cuts and sores. Food handlers who have septic cuts, boils or flu should not prepare food. Rapid cooling of high-risk foods.	Produces a toxin in foods which is difficult to destroy by normal cooking temperatures. Responsible for less than 1% of the reported cases of food poisoning.
Bacillus cereus	Cereals, particularly rice and corn flour. Cooked rice dishes. Dairy products. Spices and vegetables. Dust and soil.	Vomiting and/ or diarrhoea	Good personal and kitchen hygiene. Thorough cooking of rice and pasta. Throw cooked rice out after 24 hours. Rapid cooling of hot foods. Ensure vegetables are washed before use.	Reheating during flash frying, as in fried rice, must be thorough or else bacteria will not be destroyed. Food poisoning can often be caused by take-away rice dishes.
Clostridium botulinum	Home canning. Smoked fish. Canned or vacuum-packed foods.	Difficulty in swallowing, talking, breathing Double vision which may lead to muscle paralysis	Check that the joins of canned food are not damaged when purchasing. Air and bacteria may have entered.	A very rare form of food poisoning.

Top Tip Throw out dented, blown or out-of-date canned products.

Quick Test

1. Why are *staphylococcus* bacteria particularly linked to the food handler?
2. Why has there been an increase in reported cases of *bacillus cereus*?
3. What should you do with out-of-date canned products?
4. Unjumble the following symptoms of *salmonella* food poisoning.
   a. Raedahior b. Iigvnmot c. Mcoshat ipna d. Evref
5. *Clostridium perfringens* can be found in soil on vegetables. What must be done to vegetables to prevent the risk of this bacterium spreading?

Answers 1. They can contaminate food through touching their nose, mouth, skin, cuts and boils **2.** Increased use of 'take-away meals' containing rice **3.** Throw out **4. a.** Diarrhoea **b.** Vomiting **c.** Stomach pain **d.** Fever **5.** Careful washing of vegetables

Food-borne diseases

	Sources	Symptoms	Methods of prevention	Other information
E. coli 0157	Undercooked meat products. Contaminated cooked meats. Found in the intestines of animals and people.	Stomach pain Diarrhoea Vomiting May lead to kidney failure	Rigorous personal and food hygiene. Separate raw and cooked foods to prevent cross-contamination.	
Campylobacter	Wild birds. Untreated water. Unpasteurised milk. Raw poultry and meat. Sewage.	Diarrhoea Fever Nausea Stomach pain	Effective personal and kitchen hygiene. Thorough cooking of meat and poultry. Thorough reheating of leftovers to 82°C.	This is the most common cause of acute bacterial diarrhoea food poisoning in Scotland. Many people just put this down to an upset stomach.
Listeria	Transmitted through food, particularly soft cheese, pâté and cook-chill reheated meals.	Diarrhoea Fever	Avoid the food sources if pregnant, as the unborn child may be harmed. Also the elderly or already ill may be at risk. Chilled foods to be stored below 5°C. Reheat foods to 82°C.	
Dysentery	Faeces of infected people, flies, cockroaches. Salads, unpeeled fruit, ice cream, ice cubes.	Diarrhoea Fever Cramps Vomiting	Strict toilet and personal hygiene. Washing of fruit and vegetables to be eaten uncooked.	In certain countries, avoid foods which use local water in its preparation.
Typhoid	Water or food contaminated by faeces or urine. Flies.	Headache Tiredness High temperature Stomach pain Diarrhoea	Public-health measures, e.g. clean water supply. High standard of hygiene in the home.	Typhoid is still common in the developing world. If travelling, take precautions – drink bottled water.

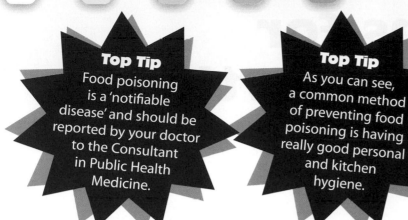

Top Tip
Food poisoning is a 'notifiable disease' and should be reported by your doctor to the Consultant in Public Health Medicine.

Top Tip
As you can see, a common method of preventing food poisoning is having really good personal and kitchen hygiene.

Incubation period

You might not develop food poisoning immediately after eating food infected with bacteria.

Each bacterium will have an incubation period. This is the time between eating the food and the first signs or the onset of illness. Each bacterium will have different onset times – some are less than others. For example, food poisoning from *staphylococcus* bacteria may start 2–4 hours after eating infected food. *Campylobacter* can be 2–5 days; *Listeria* bacteria can be 3 days to 3 weeks.

Duration of symptoms

The duration of the food-poisoning illness will vary with each bacteria and the severity of the symptoms. The symptoms of *campylobacter* food poisoning do not usually last longer than 7 days. *Bacillus cereus* food poisoning usually lasts 12–48 hours.

Quick Test

1. Which bacteria are the most common cause of acute bacterial diarrhoea food poisoning in Scotland?

2. Which food-poisoning bacteria can affect an unborn child?

3. What are the symptoms of *E. coli 0157* food poisoning?

4. Which of the following is the most likely to cause *E. coli 0157* infection?
    a. liver pâté **b.** undercooked hamburger **c.** tinned kidney beans **d.** yoghurt

5. To what temperature should leftovers be reheated?
    a. 75°C **b.** 70°C **c.** 82°C **d.** 85°C

6. Which of the following is not a food-borne disease bacterium?
    a. *E. coli* **b.** *Listeria* **c.** *Campylobacter* **d.** *Clostridium perfringens*

Answers 1. *Campylobacter* **2.** *Listeria* **3.** Stomach pain, diarrhoea, vomiting, may lead to kidney failure **4. b.** Undercooked hamburger **5. c.** 82°C **6. d.** *Clostridium perfringens*

Conditions for bacterial growth

Bacteria grow and multiply quickly in certain conditions. The four main conditions are:
1. Temperature
2. Moisture
3. Time
4. Food

1. Temperature

At 100°C   In boiling water (100°C), most bacteria are killed in 1–2 minutes.

At 82°C   It is important that any reheating of food is done thoroughly, reaching at least 82°C so that bacteria are killed.

At 63°C   Above 63°C, bacteria begin to die. This is also the temperature of hot holding of foods in a restaurant.

At 37°C   Bacteria like the warmth and prefer to live at the temperature of the human body: 37°C. This allows them to grow and multiply at a fast rate.

At 4°C   Low temperatures: 4°C (normal refrigerator temperature) will slow down or stop bacterial growth but will not kill them.

At -18°C   Very low temperatures: −18°C (normal freezer temperature) will ensure that bacteria become dormant (don't multiply) in frozen foods. However, as the food defrosts, bacteria begin to multiply again.

Hot
at or above
a min. temp.
of 63°C

63°C

danger zone

Chilled
at or below
a max. temp.
of 5°C

5°C

Top Tip
Remember
the danger zone
for encouraging
bacterial growth is
between 5°C and
63°C.

2. Moisture

Bacteria need moisture to grow and multiply.

They cannot grow in dried foods, e.g. flour, dried milk, soup powders and uncooked rice.

However, they will start to grow again when a liquid is added and left for a period of time in warm conditions.

3. Time

Given the correct conditions, bacteria will start to multiply by dividing themselves in half every twenty minutes or less. If multiplication continued, one bacterium would become over 1 million after seven hours.

4. Food

Like all living cells, bacteria need food to grow and multiply. Foods can be classed as High-Risk or Low-Risk.

High-Risk foods

Sometimes these foods are called 'perishable foods', as they can 'go off' easily. They usually require storage in a refrigerator.

They include foods:

- high in protein, e.g. meat, fish
- high in moisture, e.g. gravies, soups
- that do not require any further heating, e.g.

    - all cooked meats and poultry

    - cooked meat products including pies, sausages

    - milk, cream, artificial cream, custard and dairy produce

    - egg products such as mayonnaise

    - shellfish and sea food

    - cooked rice.

Low-Risk foods

These foods do not supply the bacteria with the conditions they require to multiply, so there is less risk of food poisoning.

They include:

- foods high in salt, e.g. savoury snacks, crisps
- foods high in sugar, e.g. jam
- foods high in acid, e.g. pickled onions
- foods high in fat, e.g. butter, lard
- dry foods, e.g. biscuits, cereals.

This is why food-preservation methods such as jam-making, salting and pickling are so successful.

Top Tip
Damp tea towels can allow bacteria to multiply easily in a warm kitchen. Change after every use or allow the dishes to air dry.

Quick Test

1. What are the main conditions bacteria require to grow?

2. What is meant by the danger zone?

3. What happens to bacteria when food is frozen?

4. What are perishable foods?

Answers 1. Temperature, moisture, time, food **2.** Bacteria can multiply rapidly between 5 and 63°C **3.** They become dormant **4.** Foods that can 'go off' easily and need to be stored in a refrigerator

Cross-contamination

Cross-contamination is the transfer of bacteria from a contaminated source to an uncontaminated food. This transfer is done through a 'vehicle'.

Top Tip
A vehicle of bacterial contamination is usually
• hands
• cloths and equipment
• surfaces.
This can be termed indirect contamination.

Bacteria

If a high-risk food is left for some time in a warm room, the few bacteria which have been transferred to it will multiply to large numbers, and, when the food is eventually eaten, it will cause food poisoning.

Here are some examples of cross-contamination:

a. using a chopping board or other kitchen equipment for the preparation of two different foods without washing it thoroughly between each use

b. the hands of a food handler which are not washed between preparing different types of food, e.g. raw and cooked meats, or after touching any source of bacteria, e.g. nose, mouth, hair, pets, or not washing hands after visiting the toilet

c. incorrect positioning of foods in a refrigerator, e.g. raw meat must always be placed below cooked foods so that blood (which contains pathogenic bacteria) cannot drip onto the cooked food

d. using a knife or other utensil without washing it thoroughly after each use.

Physical contamination

This results when bits and pieces of materials from people, animals, equipment and waste matter get into the food that people are going to eat. This type of contamination is usually large enough to be seen but might go unnoticed when it has been mixed into the food during preparation, cooking or storing. Someone could put this 'foreign body' into their mouth and even swallow it. If the kitchen and storage areas are not kept clean and tidy, and food handlers are careless in the production of food, objects that are not edible may get into food.

Examples of 'foreign bodies' are:
• stones, dirt, bones from raw materials
• human hair, small pieces of jewellery, plasters, buttons from food handlers
• plastic, paper, string from packaging materials

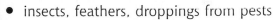

- insects, feathers, droppings from pests
- bristles, bits of cloth from cleaning materials
- screws, nuts, bits of metal from machinery used in food production.

If food contaminated in this way is sold to the public, it may result in the food business being prosecuted.

Chemical contamination

Chemicals may be put into the food in a planned way, e.g. by spraying the crops with fertiliser or weedkiller before they are harvested. Or, at other times, chemicals may be mixed with foods accidentally. There are several ways this could happen in a kitchen:

- Spray cleaner or insect sprays (called insecticides) are used where there is food uncovered.
- Pesticides (for killing mice or rats) are put down in a kitchen area where they might come into contact with food or with equipment that will be used for preparing food.
- The use of excess disinfectants and detergents can accidentally contaminate food being prepared, e.g. cleaning materials being overused in the kitchen or stored in unlabelled food-type containers such as drink bottles. There may be permanent and serious damage to the health of a person who swallows chemically contaminated food. They might even die.

Sometimes the plant and animal world can produce food which is not safe to eat. Here are a few examples:

- Potatoes – if they are green, they are poisonous and should not be eaten.
- Mushrooms – some wild mushrooms (which look parasol-shaped with white underneath) are poisonous. Be careful if you pick your own.
- Rhubarb – the leaves and the bud on the rhubarb plant are poisonous.
- Some shellfish – particularly if living in polluted waters or feeding on poisonous plants.

Top Tip
Our bodies require tiny amounts of metal to function, e.g. iron, zinc and copper, which are found naturally in many foods. However, excessive amounts of metal can be toxic (poisonous).

Quick Test

1. What is cross-contamination?
2. Name three types of food contamination.
3. While eating a shop-bought flan, you almost swallowed a button. What type of contamination is this?
4. Name three common vehicles for bacterial contamination.

Answers 1. The transfer of bacteria from a contaminated source to an uncontaminated food **2.** Bacterial, physical, chemical **3.** Physical
4. Hands, cloths and equipment; surfaces

Safe storage, preparation and serving of food

Food storage

Food must be stored correctly, according to the type of food, in order to prevent it from going off or spoiling and to keep it safe to eat.

Therefore food should be stored:

- in the right place – refrigerator, freezer or dry store
- at the right temperature
- for the correct amount of time.

Perishable foods are kept cold to:

- slow down food spoilage
- prevent the growth of food-poisoning bacteria. These foods must be stored below 5°C using either a refrigerator or a freezer.

There are certain rules which should be followed to ensure the correct use of both so that they can work effectively and efficiently and also prevent cross-contamination.

Rules for using the refrigerator (short-term storage)

- The operating temperature must be between 1°C and 4°C.
- To prevent contamination, raw and cooked foods should be stored in different areas.
- Foods must be covered, e.g. with cling film or foil, to prevent drying out or transferring odours from one food to another and to prevent direct contact between foods.
- The refrigerator must not be overloaded, or it will not operate at the correct temperature.
- Hot food must never be put into the refrigerator, as it will raise the temperature to above 5°C and put other foods at risk.
- Eggs should be kept in their box in the refrigerator.
- Left-over canned foods should be emptied into another container before being refrigerated. The chemicals in cans may cause chemical poisoning.

Rules for using the freezer (both short- and long-term storage)

- The operating temperature of the freezer should be -18°C.
- All foods must be labelled with the name and date of food.
- If food has been defrosted, it should not be refrozen unless it has been cooked first.
- Food should be packaged well to prevent it drying out and being damaged.
- Food should be frozen when it is in its best condition, as it will last longer.
- Food should not be kept any longer than the date recommended by the manufacturer.
- Defrost food in a cool place (refrigerator) in a dish or tray and allow plenty of time.

However, there are some rules which are common to both the refrigerator and freezer.

- They should be positioned in well-ventilated areas away from heat sources, e.g. ovens, sunshine.

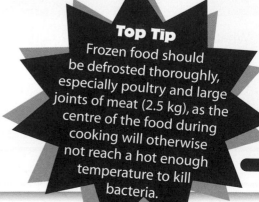

Top Tip
Frozen food should be defrosted thoroughly, especially poultry and large joints of meat (2.5 kg), as the centre of the food during cooking will otherwise not reach a hot enough temperature to kill bacteria.

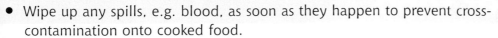

- Wipe up any spills, e.g. blood, as soon as they happen to prevent cross-contamination onto cooked food.
- Do not leave the door or lid open – food will warm up and spoil more quickly.

Rules for storing food in a dry store

Cupboards are used to store a variety of food products – canned and dried foods, packets, jars, bottles.

- A dry store should be dry, cool and well lit.
- Avoid storing dry foods in damp conditions, as mould will grow.
- It should be well ventilated and vermin-proof.
- Food should be stored off the floor and in containers. This prevents any spillages from attracting insects or mice.

Top Tip
It is important to rotate any food in stock. Always use the oldest first. First In, First Out (the FIFO system).

Labelling

Labelling on food packaging plays an important role in preventing food poisoning by ensuring that food is stored correctly.

Date marking

The most common date markings are the **Use by date** and the **Best before date**.

Use by

- Used on highly perishable and high-risk foods, e.g. meat, yoghurts.
- The food must be used by the date given, or there is a risk of food poisoning.
- After purchase, these foods could be frozen or cooked – this would extend the Use by date.

Best before

- Used on products that are less perishable, e.g. flour, pasta.
- The label means that the product is at its best for quality, flavour and texture before this date.
- Food can be eaten after this date, but it may not be at its best for quality, flavour and texture.

Quick Test

1. Name three areas used for food storage.
2. What should the temperatures be of a refrigerator and a freezer?
3. Where should eggs be stored?
4. Why should dried foods be stored off the floor?

Answers 1. Refrigerator, freezer and dry store **2.** Between 1–4°C, -18°C **3.** In their box in the refrigerator **4.** To prevent spillages from attracting insects or mice

73

Cooking of food

Apart from following the guidelines for the cold storage of foods, there are other temperatures and rules you need to know if you are to prevent the growth of food-poisoning bacteria in high-risk foods when cooking. Thorough cooking destroys harmful bacteria, and food should be cooked so that the inside or core temperature reaches 75°C.

To check this, use a disinfected food probe thermometer. The point should be pushed into the centre of the food and held for 1–3 minutes until the gauge registers the temperature. Remember to clean the pointed end afterwards so that it does not contaminate any other food.

Top Tip
Only a clean, disinfected spoon should be used for tasting food, otherwise bacteria will be spread.

Cooling of food

You may want to cool food that has been cooked so that you can serve it cold or keep it to reheat the next day.

Large pieces or amounts of food that have just been cooked and are left to cool on their own will cool very slowly, and this could cause bacteria to multiply as the temperature drops. You must get the food out of the danger zone of 5–63°C as quickly as possible by:

- placing the covered food in a cold room or store
- using a blast chiller (found in large catering establishments)
- dividing the food into small portions, covering and leaving in a cool place.

After cooling, food must be stored below 5°C.

Top Tip
Food should be covered and kept separate from raw food during the cooling process.

Reheating of food

If food has to be reheated, you must follow the rules exactly, or it could cause illness. The law requires that foods in the hospitality industry should be reheated to 82°C.

To get food out of the danger zone, you must:

- never try to reheat large pieces of food (2.5 kg)
- throw out any left-over reheated food
- never reheat a piece of food more than once.

If you want to reheat a chicken or roast meat, slice it first then reheat it in gravy.

Serving of food

There are many hazards associated with serving food which could cause food poisoning:

- Length of time food is kept at a warm temperature
- Contamination from food handlers, equipment, utensils and price tags (in shops)
- Self-service from food displays and buffets.

These rules must be followed

- Food which is kept hot prior to serving should be kept at a temperature of above 63°C to avoid multiplication of bacteria.
- Food handlers should always wear appropriate clean protective clothing and be trained in all aspects of food safety. Staff should not handle money and then touch high-risk foods.
- All equipment and utensils used for service must be in good condition, cleaned and disinfected and dry. Cutlery and cups should be held by the handles.
- Customers should not be able to handle open food. Tongs and serving spoons should be available.
- Price tags or labels should not be stuck into food.
- If cold foods, e.g. salad or sandwiches or cakes, are on sale at self-service counters, they must be kept at temperatures of below 5°C.
- They must be covered, and have a sneeze guard – this is a sheet of glass between the food and the customer.

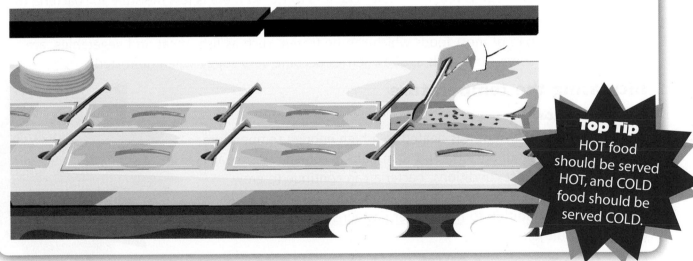

Top Tip
HOT food should be served HOT, and COLD food should be served COLD.

Quick Test

1. What temperature should food reach when being reheated?

2. What would you use to check the temperature of the centre of a chicken?

3. After food has been cooled, what temperature should it be stored at?

4. What is a sneeze guard?

5. You cooked a sweet and sour chicken for yourself. You left it in the pan in a warm kitchen for about four hours until meal time. Then you quickly warmed it up, as you did not want it so hot that it would burn your mouth. The next day, you were unwell with food poisoning. Give two reasons why you got food poisoning.

Answers 1. 82°C **2.** Probe food thermometer **3.** Below 5°C **4.** A sheet of glass between the food and the customer **5.** The food was left sitting for four hours in a warm kitchen, so bacteria multiplied; the food was not thoroughly reheated to 82°C

Food preservation

Food is preserved in order to extend its life and to stop it from spoiling. Food spoilage can be prevented by either:

- slowing down the activity of disease-causing bacteria, or
- destroying the bacteria which make the food unfit to eat.

The main ways of preserving food are by

- temperature control
- removing moisture
- using chemicals.

Temperature control

Reducing the temperature

Chilling or refrigeration

Chilled foods are extremely popular with consumers, as usually the taste and texture of the food is not changed. The temperature in a refrigerator should be below 5°C. Bacterial growth and food spoilage are slowed down but not stopped, so food will begin to spoil over time. It is important to check 'Use by' dates on perishable products such as yoghurt, milk and cooked meats.

Freezing

As temperatures are lowered during freezing to between −22°C and −18°C, bacteria become dormant, so food spoilage is reduced. Water changes to ice, so there is less moisture for bacteria to grow. However, when food defrosts, the temperature rises, allowing the bacteria to start to multiply.

The taste and texture of most foods which can be frozen, such as fish, meat and vegetables, are not affected, but some fruits such as strawberries become very soggy when defrosted.

Increasing the temperature

Pasteurisation

When food is pasteurised, it is heated to a high enough temperature to kill most but not all bacteria and then quickly cooled. This means that, given the correct conditions, bacteria can continue to grow and multiply. Pasteurised foods such as milk must be stored under refrigeration. In addition to milk, other pasteurised products include ice cream and fruit juices.

Top Tip
It is better to defrost food in the refrigerator, as the low temperature prevents the bacteria from multiplying quickly.

Ultra Heat Treatment (UHT)

Food is heated to a temperature of 135–140°C for a very short time of 1–2 seconds. This temperature destroys most bacteria and so reduces the risk of food spoiling. The most common UHT product is milk, but the process is also used for fruit juices, yoghurts and cream. UHT milk will last for 6–9 months at room temperature until opened. After opening, it must be stored under refrigeration.

Canning

Prepared food is placed into cans, heated to high temperatures of 115–125°C to destroy the bacteria, and sealed (either before or while the food is heated) to prevent any new bacteria from entering. Canned foods have a long storage time at room temperature. After opening, they should be treated as perishable foods.

Top Tip
After opening canned foods, leftovers should be stored in a plastic container in the refrigerator. Leaving leftovers in the can may result in the food absorbing a metallic taste from the can.

Removing moisture

Bacteria require moisture to multiply. Removing the water, by drying the food, means that the bacteria do not have a source of moisture which would allow them to multiply. Dehydrated foods or dried foods can be stored for quite a long time in an airtight container. Dehydrated products include powdered milk, dried potatoes, dried pasta, dried fruit, powdered soups and sauces. Once reconstituted (liquid has been added), foods should be used immediately or stored under refrigeration.

Using chemicals

Vinegar

The pickling method of preservation uses vinegar. The addition of vinegar will create acidic conditions (a pH of below 4.5), which means that bacteria cannot multiply. Foods that can be pickled include onions, cucumber, eggs and herring.

Salt

Most bacteria, with the exception of *staphylococci* and *salmonellae*, cannot multiply in high concentrations of salt. The salt dries out the food by absorbing the moisture, so there is none available for bacteria. Foods that are salted include fish and continental sausages.

Sugar

Sugar is used in large quantities in jam-making to act as a preservative by preventing the growth of bacteria. However, yeasts and mould are still able to grow on jam.

Chemicals

Chemical preservatives are added to food to prevent spoilage by either killing or reducing the activity of bacteria. The most common types are:

– nitrates and nitrites which can be used to cure meats, e.g. ham

– sulphites such as sulphur dioxide which can be used in wine, fruit juice and some meat products.

Quick Test

1. Name the methods of preservation which involve a reduction in temperature.

2. Which foods can be ultra heat treated?

3. How does salt preserve food?

4. How does drying preserve food?

Answers 1. Chilling/refrigeration and freezing **2.** Milk, yoghurt, fruit juices, cream **3.** The salt dries out the food by absorbing the moisture, so there is none available for bacteria **4.** Removing the water means that the bacteria do not have a source of moisture to allow them to multiply

The law and food safety

In order to ensure that food is safe for consumers to eat, there are laws and regulations in place which all food businesses have to follow. All places that sell food, such as supermarkets, shops, hotel, restaurants, cafés, burger vans and food stalls, are covered by these laws.

The main pieces of food-safety legislation that you need to know about are

- The Food Safety Act 1990
- The Food Hygiene (Scotland) Regulations 2006.

The Food Safety Act 1990

The main requirements of this Act are that food

- must be the nature, substance or quality described, e.g. haddock should be haddock and not cod
- must not be falsely or misleadingly described or labelled, e.g. eggs from a battery-reared chicken should not be described as 'free range'
- must not cause injury to health
- must not be unfit to use or contaminated, e.g. chicken that has decomposed and gone 'off' and smells.

Top Tip
This Act applies to all the food premises that are involved in the production, processing, storage, distribution or sale of food.

Anyone who runs a food business has to register with their local authority. This means that the local authority can monitor all the food-production businesses and inspect them regularly.

Environmental Health Officers (EHOs)

EHOs are employed by the local authority; they visit food premises and enforce the requirements of the Food Safety Act 1990 and the Food Hygiene (Scotland) Regulations 2006.

- Should a food business not be meeting the requirements of food-safety legislation, then the EHOs can seize and remove food which is regarded as unfit to eat.
- Failure to comply with food-hygiene regulations may result in the service of an improvement notice, which states how a business is failing to meet the requirements of the Act, the improvements required and the time allowed to make the improvements.
- If the officer is satisfied that there is a real risk of injury to health, an emergency prohibition notice may be served, and this could mean that the premises would be closed immediately, or a certain piece of equipment or process must not be used.
- The next stage is for the EHO to apply to court for an emergency prohibition order. When all the improvements have been carried out, a certificate is given to the food business, and it can reopen for business.

'Due diligence'

If a food business is charged with an offence under the Food Safety Act 1990, then it can use the defence of 'due diligence'. This allows the defendant possibly to be acquitted of an offence if they prove that they 'took all reasonable precautions and exercised all due diligence to avoid committing the offence'.

To prove that reasonable precautions have been taken involves setting up a system of procedures and controls and checking that these systems are operated properly. Clear, written records should be kept.

The Food Hygiene (Scotland) Regulations 2006

These regulations are based on European Union food-safety laws which state certain safety standards for the processing and sale of foods.

These regulations apply to food businesses, so ensuring that all stages of food production are carried out in a hygienic way, food handlers are trained, and good structural standards are in place in the food premises. Consumers are therefore assured of food safe to eat.

From January 2006, food businesses must have in place a Hazard Analysis Critical Control Point (HACCP) system. With the HACCP system, the food producer has to

- identify possible food-safety risks or **hazards**
- put **control measures** in place to prevent or control these hazards. Some control measures are called critical control points. These are the stages during food production where it is critical that the hazard be controlled so that the food is safe to eat.
- make sure these controls are monitored and action may have to be taken to correct any failings in procedures
- review all the HACCP procedures on a regular basis
- keep records. Keeping records is an important part of HACCP, as this will provide evidence of all the procedures that are in place.

The regulations also cover temperature control. Temperature is an important factor in the prevention of bacterial multiplication during food production.

The law states that food must
- be kept refrigerated
- be kept in a cool ventilated place
- be kept at a holding temperature above 63°C
- if being reheated, be kept at 82°C or above.

Top Tip
A hazard could be cross-contamination by food-poisoning bacteria, e.g. storing raw meat next to cooked foods.

Top Tip
The control measure would be: separate raw and cooked foods during storage.

Quick Test

1. Name the two most important pieces of food-safety legislation.

2. Name two physical hazards.

3. What does the abbreviation HACCP stand for?

4. What is a critical control point?

Answers 1. The Food Safety Act 1990 and the Food Hygiene (Scotland) Regulations 2006 2. Glass, buttons 3. Hazard Analysis Critical Control Point 4. These are the stages during food production where it is critical that the hazard be controlled so that the food is safe to eat.

The Food Hygiene (Scotland) Regulations 2006 also make specific rules and regulations about the design of all food premises, whether a restaurant, mobile burger van or vending machines. Some of the main points are explained below.

The food premises

- The layout and design should allow for easy cleaning and disinfecting.
- Floors should be easy to clean, non-absorbent and non-slip. There should be no gaps at the join between the wall and floor, as this space can develop a build-up of dirt and bacteria.
- Walls and ceiling should be smooth and light in colour, so spillages or dirt are seen and easy to clean.
- Windows which can open should be fitted with a insect-proof screen which can then be easily cleaned.

Surfaces and equipment

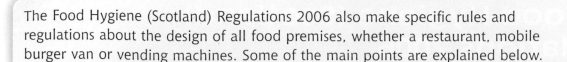

- Equipment should be designed and constructed so that dirt and bacteria can be destroyed by thorough cleaning and disinfecting.
- Work surfaces should be easy to clean and disinfect and smooth to ensure that no bacteria or dirt can be trapped.
- Surfaces and equipment which come into contact with both raw and cooked foods should be cleaned well before and after use.
- Equipment should be easy to move so that cleaning is made easier.

Ventilation and lighting

- Ventilation should be such that there is not a build-up of heat or moisture which would encourage the growth of bacteria.
- Lighting should be good so there are no dark areas which could be missed during the cleaning process. Pests like dark areas.
- For safety, good lighting is important when working with dangerous

Top Tip
Stainless steel is long-lasting and easily cleaned, so is often used for food-preparation equipment and surfaces.

Food workers

- Food workers should be trained and supervised in food-hygiene procedures.
- They should have good personal hygiene and wear clean, protective clothing.
- They should not prepare food if suffering from colds, coughs, sickness or diarrhoea, or they have cuts or boils.
- Food workers could be unaware that they could be 'carriers' of food poisoning bacteria. They may not show any signs of illness themselves but could pass on food-poisoning bacteria to others.

Changing facilities

- When staff have to change into protective clothing, changing facilities of a suitable size, with lockers to store outdoor clothing, and seating, should be provided. This ensures that the staff can change without getting their protective clothing dirty.

Water supply

- The water supply should be potable (drinkable) and in good supply.

Wash hand basins

- Wash hand basins should have good supplies of hot and cold water, soap and hand-drying facilities.
- Wash hand basins should only be used for washing hands, not for any food preparation.

Hand washing
ONLY

Toilets

- The number of toilets should be sufficient for the number of employees.
- They should not open directly onto areas where food is prepared.
- There should be good ventilation.

Food waste

- Food waste should be disposed of regularly and not allowed to build up in the food-preparation area. This will help pest control.
- Store in easy-to-clean and easy-to-disinfect containers with a closable lid.

Top Tip
Throughout all of your practical work, it is good practice to wash your hands after disposing of food waste – this shows good hygiene, which will earn you marks.

Pest control

- Pests such as rodents (mice and rats), insects (flies, wasps, bluebottles, cockroaches and ants) and birds all carry dirt, disease and bacteria.
- Signs of pest infestation include mice droppings, live or dead bodies, damage such as gnawing marks on packaging or food, unusual smells, footprints and tail marks in dust or flour.
- Food premises can control flies by installing an electric fly-killer or having a self-closing exit door.

Quick Test

1. Why should the join between the floor and wall be smooth in a food-preparation kitchen?
2. Why should there be good lighting in a food-preparation area?
3. When should food workers not be involved in food preparation?
4. What does the word infestation mean?

Answers 1. To prevent a build-up of dirt and bacteria **2.** So there are no dark areas which could be missed during the cleaning process and also for safety when working with dangerous equipment **3.** If suffering from colds, coughs, sickness or diarrhoea, or they have cuts or boils **4.** The premises can be overrun by pests

Cleaning procedures

Cleaning

Clean food premises, equipment and work surfaces are very important to all food businesses. Good hygiene and cleanliness are important to a food business because:

- the health of consumers may be affected by food poisoning
- the reputation of a food business depends on clean premises and hygienic food
- equipment will work better and last longer if properly cleaned and cared for.

Cleaning schedule

Environmental Health Officers may visit and inspect a food business at any time and request to see the records of cleaning schedules applied by the food business.

A cleaning schedule usually provides information about:

- the area or items to be cleaned and how often they have to be cleaned
- the method of cleaning used
- the date when cleaning was last done
- the signature of the person responsible for the cleaning

The items requiring to be cleaned or disinfected include all that come into contact with food, for example cooking utensils, crockery and cutlery, food-preparation equipment, work surfaces, pans, cookers, sinks, wash basins, refuse waste bins.

	Mon	Tue	Wed	Thu	Fri	Sat	Sun
walk-in fridges	DM	RG	GB	RG	RG	RG	GB
stove tops	DM	RG	EI	EI	DM	RG	GB
shelves	DM	EI	GB	EI	DM	EI	GB
work surfaces	EI	EI	GB	EI	GB	EI	GB
walls	DM	EI	EI	DM	GB	EI	DM
floor	EI	RG	GB	DM	RG	RG	DM
extractor hood	EI	RG	GB	DM	RG	RG	DM

There are two main ways of achieving hygienically clean surfaces, equipment and cloths.

Heat

Using very hot water will destroy bacteria. Dishwashers are used in the food industry, as they sterilise dishes.

Chemicals

Either:

1. a bactericidal detergent, which is a combined cleaner and bactericide designed to remove dirt and destroy bacteria, or

2. a detergent to remove dirt, followed by a disinfectant which will reduce bacteria to a safe level.

In the catering industry, the following procedure is followed:

1. Pre-clean – removing excess dirt by brushing or wiping

2. Main clean – loosening of the surface grease and dirt using a detergent

3. Rinse – removal of loose dirt and detergent

4. Disinfection – destroying bacteria

5. Final rinse – removal of disinfection

6. Drying – this should be done naturally.

Top Tip
Staff in food premises should be trained to 'clean as you go'. This means cleaning up after one job before starting on a new task.

Top Tip
Disinfectants need time to work, so it is important to allow sufficient contact time to allow the disinfectant to work well.

Key terms in food hygiene

Carrier – a food worker who could be unaware that they are infected with particular food-poisoning bacteria. They may show no signs of illness themselves but can carry or pass on the food-poisoning bacteria to other people.

Cleaning – the process when detergent is used to clean and remove dirt, grease, food residue and some bacteria.

Cross-contamination – the transfer of bacteria from a contaminated source to an uncontaminated food.

Detergent – a chemical that should remove dirt and grease.

Disinfectant – a chemical that is used in the cleaning process to reduce food-poisoning and food-spoilage bacteria to a level such that food will be safe for people to eat.

Disinfection – the process of reducing micro-organisms to a safe level by using heat (hot water at about 82°C, or steam) or a disinfectant.

Food-borne illness – an infection caused by the consumption of food contaminated by micro-organisms which do not need to multiply within the food to cause illness.

Food contamination – the infection or spoilage of food or the food environment by bacteria, making the food dangerous to eat.

Food hygiene – all practices necessary to ensure that food will be acceptable and safe to eat, so preventing contamination of food.

Food poisoning – an illness caused by eating contaminated or poisonous food.

Food spoilage – the change in food or damage done to food which makes it unsafe to eat.

Pathogenic bacteria – bacteria which are harmful to humans and cause disease or illness.

Sanitisers/bactericidal detergent – combines a detergent and disinfectant and can be used on surfaces to clean and disinfect.

Spore – a resting phase of bacteria when they do not multiply, and some are able to survive conditions such as high temperatures and freezing.

Toxins – poisons produced by some micro-organisms which are harmful and cause illness.

Vehicle – the transfer or movement of bacteria from a contaminated source to an uncontaminated food is done through a 'vehicle' such as unwashed hands.

Quick Test

1. Why is good hygiene important to a food business?
2. Who may inspect a food business?
3. What is the definition of 'cleaning'?

Answers 1. The health of consumers may be affected by food poisoning OR The reputation of a food business depends on clean premises and hygienic food OR Equipment will work better and last longer if properly cleaned and cared for **2.** Environmental Health Officer **3.** The process when detergent is used to clean and remove dirt, grease, food residue and some bacteria

Evaluate your practical work

After you have completed your practical work, it is useful to evaluate how you got on. This will give you an idea of areas you could improve and areas you are already doing well in.

How to self-assess

Before you start, think about:

- the important hygiene points
- the important safety points
- two or more skills in the recipe that you would like to concentrate on.

Look at the following checklist **before** you start. This will give you some ideas of areas to evaluate later. You will record your performance by ticking one of the three columns: Good, OK or Could be better.

Either copy the one below or download one from the Learning Lab section of Leckie and Leckie's website.

EVALUATION CHECKLIST

Hygiene

Activity	Good	OK	Could be better
1. Wash hands when required			
2. Hair tied back if long			
3. Jewellery removed			
4. Apron used			
5. No nail polish			
6. Fruit and vegetables washed			
7. Peelings on a paper towel			
8. Waste disposed of in bin			
9. Unit top kept clean and tidy			
10. Dishes washed thoroughly			
11. No touching of skin or hair during practical work			
12. Clean teaspoon to taste			

Safety

Activity	Good	OK	Could be better
1. Pan handles turned in			
2. Correct oven procedure			
3. Use of oven gloves			
4. Knives used safely			
5. Equipment used safely			
6. Cooker turned off when finished			

Skills

Skills	Good	OK	Could be better
1.			
2.			
3.			

How did you get on?

After you have completed the evaluation checklist, think about

- What did you do well?
- What could you do better?
- What was your main problem, if any?
- What are your 'next steps' to improve further?

Top Tip
The best advice is to be well organised. Do not leave anything to chance. 'Practice makes perfect.'

Assessment practice

To help you pass the assessment for Food Hygiene for the Hospitality Industry, complete the following activities.

The following exercises require you to read about outbreaks of food poisoning and then answer the questions that follow. (Answers are on page 95.)

Case Study A: The 21st Birthday Party

A 21st birthday celebration was held in an Edinburgh hotel on 25 July. A cold buffet had been prepared which included cold chicken with salad dishes. This was followed by a variety of desserts including trifle. The buffet was set out, uncovered, in the early afternoon; and, because it was so hot, a member of staff decided to open the window. One hundred guests ate the cold buffet.

A number of days later, the Consultant in Public Health Medicine was notified of ten cases of food poisoning – all ten people had been at the 21st birthday party. This was proved to be caused by *salmonella* bacteria in the trifle.

On investigation, he found that the chickens had been defrosted on the top shelf of the fridge, with the decorated trifle placed on the shelf below.

Questions

1. Give two reasons why the *salmonella* was found in the trifle. (2)
2. Is there anything significant about the date? (1)
3. Suggest four actions that the hotel should take to prevent further outbreaks of food poisoning. (4)
4. If one of the salad dishes contained rice, what advice would you give the chef to ensure it was safe to eat? (3)

10 marks

Case Study B: The Canteen Lunch

A food handler in a works canteen prepared a large pot of custard, which was usually served with a variety of puddings most days.

He finished making it at 10 o'clock and left it to cool. He thought he had forgotten to add sugar, so tasted it with a wooden spoon to see if that was the case. He added sugar, and with the same wooden spoon tasted again.

The custard was left sitting in a warm kitchen until 12:30 pm, warmed up very slowly and served at 1 o'clock.

By tea time, some employees who had eaten the custard either started being sick or had stomach pains and diarrhoea.

An outbreak of *staphylococcus* food poisoning was later confirmed by the Environmental Health Officer.

Questions

1. How do you think the *staphylococcus* bacteria were passed from the food handler to the custard? (2)

2. In people, where are the four main sources of *staphylococcus*? (4)

3. When do you think these bacteria were allowed to multiply so much in the custard that they caused food poisoning? (1)

4. How do you think the food-poisoning outbreak could have been prevented? (1)

5. Name two food sources which would encourage the growth of *staphylococcus* bacteria. (2)

10 marks

Case Study C: The Take-Away Outbreak

On Friday, Bob and Harry, having been to a concert, decided to have a Chinese take-away for supper back at Bob's house. They did not finish it all, so put what was left of the rice dish back in the fridge.

On Sunday, after playing football in the afternoon, Bob decided he would reheat the Chinese food for his tea. Within three hours, he was being violently sick, had diarrhoea and became extremely dehydrated. His mother called the doctor, who recognised *bacillus cereus* food poisoning.

The food-poisoning outbreak could have been from:

1. The Chinese take-away – large quantities of rice may be boiled the day before they are required and are sometimes left in a large colander prior to preparing some Chinese dishes. This is because refrigeration is said to make the rice thick and sticky. This rice may be fried at a high temperature and kept warm before it is quickly tossed in hot fat in a final process.

2. Bob, who kept the cooked rice longer than 24 hours in the fridge and then reheated it before eating.

Questions

1. Give two ways in which the Chinese take-away could have been responsible for the food poisoning. (2)

2. Give two ways in which Bob could have been responsible for the food poisoning. (2)

3. State two ways that food can be reheated to 82°C safely. (2)

4. What advice would you have given Bob regarding his left-over Chinese meal? (1)

5. Describe three ways in which the Chinese take-away business would have to ensure the cleanliness of their food premises. (3)

10 marks

Assessment practice

You will be required to answer 20 multiple-choice questions, each worth one mark.

Here are some practice questions. For each question, write down the letter which you think provides the correct answer.

1. Which of the following contains all the necessary conditions for bacteria to grow?
   - **a.** time, warmth, food, dirt
   - **b.** food, moisture, warmth, time
   - **c.** moisture, grease, warmth, time
   - **d.** food, grease, warmth, time

2. State the ideal temperature for bacterial multiplication.
   - **a.** 50°C
   - **b.** 37°C
   - **c.** 5°C
   - **d.** 20°C

3. A micro-organism that causes food poisoning is known as
   - **a.** a spore
   - **b.** a mould
   - **c.** yeast
   - **d.** a pathogen

4. Which of the following groups is most vulnerable to food poisoning?
   - **a.** a food worker
   - **b.** a middle-aged woman
   - **c.** a baby
   - **d.** a teenager

5. Which of the following is most likely to be associated with *clostridium botulinum* poisoning?
   - **a.** mayonnaise
   - **b.** semi-skimmed milk
   - **c.** apples
   - **d.** tinned beef

6. Food contaminated by food-poisoning bacteria usually
   - **a.** looks, tastes and smells normal
   - **b.** changes colour and taste
   - **c.** smells and tastes off
   - **d.** looks and smells bad but tastes normal

7. The main reason for having high standards of cleanliness and hygiene in food premises is
   - **a.** to encourage customers
   - **b.** to make conditions more pleasurable for staff to work in
   - **c.** to make a profit
   - **d.** to protect customers from food poisoning

8. Which of the following is most likely to cause *listeria* food poisoning?
   - **a.** soft cheese
   - **b.** banana
   - **c.** canned sardines
   - **d.** beef curry

9. Most bacteria on food are killed by
   - **a.** holding food below 10°C
   - **b.** holding food above 50°C
   - **c.** heating food to 100°C
   - **d.** freezing food at -10°C

10. Which of the following should be cleaned and disinfected each day?
    - **a.** walls
    - **b.** work surfaces
    - **c.** floors
    - **d.** windows

11. If food has to be reheated, it should reach a core temperature of at least
    - **a.** 62°C
    - **b.** 72°C
    - **c.** 82°C
    - **d.** 92°C

12. It is important that any dry food storage areas are kept
   a. dry, cool, dark
   b. cool, dry, well ventilated, vermin-proof
   c. dry, vermin-proof, dark
   d. cool, airtight, well lit

13. The procedure of all food handlers should be
   a. clean at the start
   b. clean at the end
   c. clean after each dish
   d. clean as they go

14. Which of the following is a vehicle for bacterial contamination?
   a. raw food
   b. clothes and equipment
   c. refuse
   d. dust

15. What is the correct procedure for stock rotation?
   a. last in, first out
   b. last in, first use
   c. first in, last out
   d. first in, first out

16. A spore is:
   a. a resistant phase or resting phase of bacteria
   b. a microscopic plant that appears on some foods
   c. bacteria whose presence can show poor hygiene
   d. a disease which can pass from animal to human

17. A disinfectant for use in a kitchen should be
   a. odourless and non-toxic
   b. easy to use and inexpensive
   c. toxic and non-staining
   d. non-corrosive and pleasant-smelling

18. Equipment and utensils which have cracks or chips should be
   a. cleaned with a bactericide after each use
   b. only used in an emergency
   c. thrown out and replaced
   d. only used for one type of food

19. Which of the following must a food handler report to the supervisor?
   a. headache
   b. earache
   c. cramp
   d. diarrhoea

20. Open cans of food should be:
   a. placed in the refrigerator
   b. covered with cling film
   c. emptied into a container and placed in the refrigerator
   d. covered and placed in the refrigerator

Now check your answers on page 95.

How to do well in your practical assignment

To achieve the SQA Course award, you will have to plan and complete a practical assignment. In the assignment, you will use all the skills – planning, preparation, cooking and serving – that you have learned during the course of the four units of the Hospitality: Practical Cookery Intermediate 1 course.

The practical assignment for the Hospitality: Practical Cookery Intermediate 1 course is worth 70 marks and consists of two parts:

- Planning – 5 marks
- Preparing, cooking and serving food – 65 marks

Two dishes – either a starter and main course or a main course and dessert – have to be prepared in 1 ½ hours. Each dish is for four portions.

Planning

All your planning will be completed in a Planning booklet which is issued by SQA.

Plan of work

In this booklet, you have to complete a plan of work. It will show how you intend to use the 1 ½ hours on the day of your practical assignment to complete the two dishes issued by SQA.

Preparation time

Before you start to plan, there are certain preparations you are allowed to do during preparation time – this is usually ½ hour before you start your practical assignment.

The preparation time is important to allow you to get organised and be calm before you start.

Remember: these preparations should not be included in your plan of work.

What are you allowed to prepare before you start the practical assignment?

You will be allowed to 'set up' your own personal work area with all the equipment needed for preparing, cooking and serving of the foods.

The oven can be preheated during preparation time, but you must turn it off before you start the practical assignment.

Weighing and measuring can be done in advance, but preparation of raw ingredients is not allowed, e.g. peeling of vegetables.

If you want to prepare any extra garnishes or decorations, you can do this in the preparation time unless the recipe states 'prepare garnish'.

Where an ingredient states 'finely chopped parsley', this can be prepared during your preparation time.

Fresh herbs can have leaves picked from the stalk.

Top Tip

You are allowed to practise each of your dishes once in school. You should do this before you do your plan of work, as you can make notes on the recipe to show how long you took for each stage of the recipe. This will give you a rough idea of how long you will take to do each activity.

Starting your plan of work

You will be awarded the full 5 marks if your plan is in a logical order and you have managed to do this on your own.

It must show the sequence in which you are going to carry out all the activities involved in the production of the two dishes.

Use the following list to ensure that your plan of work contains all the required information.

Plan of work – CHECK

Top Tip

Plans of work and recipes can be highlighted with highlighter pens, underlined or colour coded – this will help you focus on certain important activities or times, e.g. when to take a sponge out of the oven. Use a different colour for each course – starter, main course or sweet – as this makes it even clearer.

- Indicate the start and finish times clearly.
- Allow a few minutes at the beginning of the plan to carry out personal-hygiene preparations.
- Include turning on and switching off the oven when finished.
- It is easier to plan if you break the timings of your activities into 5, 10 or 15-minute blocks.
- Check you have allowed enough time for various activities, e.g. vegetable preparation, browning of meat.
- Check the cooking time of each dish and allow the correct length of time.
- Check the serving times of your dishes. You may have to work backwards from these to make sure your dishes have sufficient time to cook.
- Correct serving times must be clearly indicated on your plan of work. The dishes have to be served in the same order as they are eaten and at specific times, e.g.

  Soup must be served 15 minutes before the end of the session
  Main course must be served 5 minutes before the end

  OR

  Main course must be served 15 minutes before the end of the session
  Dessert must be served 5 minutes before the end.
- Remember to show when you are heating or chilling your serving dishes.
- When you are testing your food for readiness, e.g. testing pasta, this must also be clearly indicated.
- Allow time to chill foods if dishes have to be served cold.
- Include putting food into the refrigerator – this shows good food hygiene.
- Check that you have included all the activities in the recipe. You don't have to write out each exact detail of your recipe. For example, you may want to include 'Whisk cream, cover, refrigerate' instead of writing out each detailed step from the recipe.
- Include the cut of vegetable, e.g. dice, slice – this will remind you to do it correctly.
- Tasting the dish and checking for seasoning should be included.
- State the times for washing dishes and tidying – clean as you go will earn you more marks!

Equipment list

You have to complete an equipment list. This is not awarded any marks but is useful as a reminder of the equipment you may need to collect.

Preparing, cooking and serving food

Your teacher will be observing you as you work, so it is important you do your best. You will gain marks for everything you do correctly.

Awarding of marks

Marks are awarded under three main areas.

Area 1. Working methods
This includes

1. Basic preparation skills and techniques
This could include marks awarded for:

– accurate weighing and measuring of ingredients: remember to re-weigh your prepared fruit and vegetables

– knife skills: using knives correctly and competently.

2. Flow of the work plan

– You should follow your plan of work as you have written it.

– Try to stick to your timings as accurately as possible.

– If you fall behind, do not panic! Keep working steadily, and you will catch up.

3. Control of cookery processes
You must show that you are controlling and monitoring the cookery processes involved in the production of the two dishes. The processes will depend on the recipe but could include:

– simmering of a soup, not boiling

– frying vegetables without colouring them

– sauce simmered correctly

– cooking of rice by boiling

– control of oven temperature for baking blind/baking a scone base

– control of oven temperature when baking a sponge.

Area 2. Dishes produced
The marks awarded will depend on the skills covered by the recipe but could include:

1. Preparing ingredients
For example

- preparation of flan – rubbing in, consistency of pastry dough, lining of flan ring
- preparation of filling – dicing onion, slicing mushrooms, crushing garlic

- beating of sponge mixture.

2. Cooking of dish

For example

- frying of ingredients correctly
- rice drained after cooking
- adding ingredients at the correct stage of the recipe
- accurate timing of stages of the recipe
- tasting of dish.

3. Finished result

For example

- serving on a clean dish which is the correct temperature – hot, warm, room temperature or cold. If you spill, wipe the serving plate immediately before placing on the serving area.
- neat, attractive appearance of dish
- correct texture, e.g. of pastry, sponge, rice
- appropriate garnish or decoration. The garnish or decoration should not be overpowering.
- taste – well flavoured, lacking in flavour.

Area 3. Professional practice

1. Observing safety

For example

- handling sharp knives or equipment
- using a damp cloth or paper towel under the chopping board so that the board does not move when chopping
- assembling, using and washing electrical equipment
- correct, safe oven procedure
- safe use of hobs, e.g. turn off when finished
- use of oven gloves.

Top Tip
Take care if adding salt. If you add too much, you cannot remove it! Add salt gradually, and taste before you decide if you need more.

2. Observing hygiene (personal and kitchen)

For example

- wash hands before starting the practical assignment and especially after handling high-risk foods
- remove all jewellery before starting the assignment – earrings, rings, watches
- wear clean, protective clothing
- hair tied back or covered
- nail polish removed
- avoid touching hair or skin during practical work
- cuts covered
- no coughing or sneezing over food
- tasting food with a clean teaspoon
- perishable food should be covered and stored in a refrigerator
- separate chopping boards must be used for raw and cooked products
- a 'clean as you go' approach to your work – do not allow a large build-up of dishes.

Introduction to Food-Preparation Techniques (pages 26–27)

1.

Ingredients	Weighing or measuring equipment to be used
Margarine	Manual or electronic scales. Block of margarine may have been cut into 25 or 50 g units.
Water	15 ml measuring spoon
Flour	Manual or electronic scales
Chives	5 ml measuring spoon
Milk	Measuring jug

2.

Food-preparation techniques	Equipment which could be used for each technique in the recipe
1 Sieve	Plastic or metal sieve
2 Mix (pastry)	Round-bladed knife
3 Knead	Flour dredger and hands

Food-preparation techniques	Equipment which could be used for each technique in the recipe
4 Roll out	Flour dredger, rolling pin
5 Line	Rolling pin or hands for lifting
6 Trim	Rolling pin or round-bladed knife
7 Grate	All-purpose, rotary, rasp or flat grater
8 Chop	Cook's knife, vegetable knife or kitchen scissors
9 Whisk	Rotary, balloon whisk
10 Mix (egg mixture)	Fork

3.
a. Pipe – piping bag, piping nozzle
b. Cream – mixing bowl and wooden spoon, hand-held electric whisk, food processor
c. Whisk – rotary whisk, flat whisk, hand-held electric whisk, balloon whisk

4. a. parsley b. fish slice c. tablespoon, measure d. creaming e. beat f. coat g. palette h. line

Introduction to Cookery Processes (pages 48–49)

1.

Cookery process	Suitable foods
Boiling	potatoes, chicken, eggs, pasta, turnip, rice
Poaching	fish, tomatoes, eggs, apples, apricots
Steaming	fish, tomatoes, eggs, apples, apricots
Stewing	fish, tomatoes, steak, chicken, apples, turnip, apricots, pork
Baking	scones, fish, tomatoes, potatoes, steak, chicken, apples, rice, apricots, sponge
Grilling	fish, tomatoes, steak, chicken, pork
Shallow frying	fish, tomatoes, potatoes, steak, chicken, eggs, apples, rice, pork

Food	Test for readiness
Boiled potatoes	They can be easily pierced with a fork and feel soft when firm pressure is applied.
Poached pears	They can be easily pierced with a fork or skewer and feel soft when firm pressure is applied.
Steamed broccoli	They resist slightly when pierced with a fork. They should be tender but still be crisp when served.
Boiled pasta	It is cooked to the stage known as 'al dente', meaning that there should be a slight firmness or bite to it when you taste it. It looks slightly swollen with water.
Baked sponge flan	The sponge is golden brown, well risen and springy to touch. The mixture should have shrunk away slightly from the edge of the tin.
A whole roast chicken	Use a skewer to pierce the thigh of a whole chicken. When juices run clear and not pink, the chicken is cooked.
Grilled fish	Insert the tip of a thin-bladed knife or skewer easily into the thickest part of the fish. The fish appears white in colour or opaque. The flesh of the fish can easily 'flake' or come away from the bone of the fish.
Boiled rice	The rice can be tested by carefully eating a small rice grain, and it should not feel grainy or hard. The rice can also be tested by gently squeezing a grain between your fingers, and it should not feel grainy. The rice looks slightly swollen and fluffy.
Baked fruit cake	A warmed skewer is inserted into the centre of a fruit cake; if it comes out clean, the cake is ready.
Apple pie	The base of the pastry is firm and the pastry is golden brown.

2.
a. Boiling – a temperature of 100 °C with bubbles all over the surface of the pan
Simmering – at a temperature of below 100 °C with bubbles at one side of the pan
b. Below boiling point (73–93 °C), and this helps food keep its shape better
c. To protect them from the steam and prevent them from becoming soggy
d. To prevent the meat from becoming tough
e. Place the baking tray on the cooker hob.
Open the oven door fully.
Using oven gloves, place the baking tray in the oven safely.
f. To prevent burning the outside of the food and to make sure the centre of the food is thoroughly cooked
g. Cover the pan with a tight-fitting lid, damp tea towel or fire blanket to exclude the oxygen.
Leave it to cool before moving it.
Call the fire brigade if the fire gets out of control.

Organisation of Practical Skills (pages 58–59)

1. **a.** List the component parts.
   25 g sultanas, 50 g oatmeal, 75 g wheat flakes, 100 g margarine, 75 g demerara sugar
   b. How many processes does this recipe have? – 10
   Collect, weigh, mix, grease, melt, spoon, press down, bake, cut

2. Recipe: Potato, Ham and Leek Soup
   FOOD REQUISITION SHEET

	Quantity		Quantity
Meat Back bacon	75 g	Vegetables Potatoes Leek Onion	450 g 150 g 50 g
Fish		Fruit	
Dairy Low-fat cream	50 ml	Dry stores Ham stock cube Salt Pepper	½ 2.5 ml pinch
Other equipment/resources required Hand blender Meat scissors			

3. Recipe: Spicy Chicken Pasta
   FOOD REQUISITION SHEET

	Quantity		Quantity
Meat Cooked chicken	100 g	Vegetables Onion Garlic Frozen peas	50 g 1 clove 25 g
Fish		Fruit	
Dairy Margarine Low-fat yoghurt	12.5 g 15 ml	Dry stores Pasta shells Sultanas Sweetcorn (tinned) Curry powder Ground ginger Plain flour Chicken stock cube Chutney	75 g 25 g 25 g 10 ml 2.5 ml 15 ml ½ 15 ml
Other equipment/resources required Garlic crusher			

Food Hygiene for the Hospitality Industry (pages 86–89)

Case Study A: The 21st Birthday Party – Answers

1. The defrosting chicken dripped onto the trifle below.
   The food uncovered meant that flies could land on the trifle.

2. July – temperatures will be high. Bacteria can multiply very fast in a warm room.

3. Chickens must be thoroughly defrosted at the bottom of the fridge.
   Chickens must be thoroughly cooked.
   Prepared foods should not be left uncovered.
   Prepared foods should not be left in warm conditions.
   Prepared foods should be stored in a refrigerator.
   Meats and desserts should be stored in separate refrigerators.

4. Rice should be cooked on the day it is to be eaten.
   No left-over rice should be used for a salad.
   If cooked rice is over 24 hours old, then it must be thrown out.
   All cooked rice should be thrown out if uneaten.
   It should have been stored in a refrigerator until served.
   After cooking, rice should be rapidly cooled.

Case Study B: The Canteen Lunch – Answers

1. The canteen worker tasted the custard with a wooden spoon, and then used the same spoon to taste again.
   The staphylococcus bacteria were present in his mouth and passed to the custard from the spoon.

2. Human nose, mouth, skin, cuts, boils.

3. When it was sitting in the warm kitchen OR
   The custard was only warmed up before serving, therefore the toxin would be present in large quantities OR
   The bacteria and/or toxins would not be killed, as the custard was not thoroughly reheated to the correct temperature.

4. By using a clean spoon when tasting the custard
   By refrigerating the custard after cooling
   By reheating to 82 °C

5. Protein foods – milk, cream, cooked meats, eggs, fish products; any high-risk food acceptable

Case Study C: The Take-Away Outbreak – Answers

1. The rice preparation was done over many hours – boiling, cooling, frying and keeping warm – so
   – spores may have formed which could withstand high temperatures
   – yesterday's rice being left overnight unrefrigerated could cause bacteria to multiply and cause food poisoning
   – keeping rice warm could allow bacteria to multiply and cause food poisoning.

2. Bob should not have reheated the rice, as more than 24 hours had elapsed.
   After 24 hours, cooked rice should be thrown out.
   Bob may not have reheated the rice to 82 °C.
   Never reheat rice or meat dishes more than once. As the rice had been reheated already in the take-away, Bob should have thrown the leftovers out immediately.

3. In the microwave or oven

4. Throw it out

5. The layout and design should allow for easy cleaning and disinfecting:
   • Floors should be easy to clean, non-absorbent and with no gaps at the wall and floor join.
   • Walls and ceiling should be smooth to allow for easy cleaning.
   • Windows which open should be fitted with a insect-proof screen which can be cleaned.

Multiple-choice questions (pages 88–89)

1. b 2. b 3. d 4. c 5. d 6. a 7. d 8. a 9. c 10. b 11. c 12. b 13. d 14. b 15. d 16. a 17. a 18. c 19. d 20. c

Intermediate 1 Hospitality
Index